REAL

REAL
ENGLISH
AUTHENTIC
LEARNING

SKILLS BOOK 2

SECOND EDITION

SANDRA COLE

Development and authoring of
(i+) Interactive online workshops and
supplementary web material
Sandra Cole

Buy online or at the bookstore
Always quick and easy!
www.cheneliere.ca

CHENELIĒRE ÉDUCATION

REAL, Real English Authentic Learning
REAL Skills Book 2, Second Edition

Sandra Cole

© 2014 TC Media Books Inc.
© 2009 Chenelière Education Inc.

Managing Editor: Melissa Repas
Editor: Jennifer McMorran
Project Manager: Valérie Côté
Researchers: Rachel Irwin, Tara Smith
Copy Editor: Jeanine Floyd
Proofreader: Nancy Perreault
Cover and Book Designer: Micheline Roy

Web Material Editor: Jennifer McMorran
Web Material Project Manager: Solange Lemaitre-Provost

**Bibliothèque et Archives nationales du Québec and
Library and Archives Canada cataloguing in publication**

Cole, Sandra, 1971-

REAL: Real English Authentic Learning. Skills Book 2

Second Edition

For college students.

ISBN 978-2-7650-4508-3

1. English language – Textbooks for second language learners. 2. English language – Problems, exercises, etc. 3. English language – Spoken English – Problems, exercises, etc. I. Title.

PE1128.C57 2014   428.3'4   C2014-940541-3

CHENELIÈRE
ÉDUCATION

5800 rue Saint-Denis, Suite 900
Montréal (Québec) H2S 3L5 Canada
Telephone: 514 273-1066
Fax: 514 276-0324 / 1 800 814-0324
info@cheneliere.ca

ISBN 978-2-7650-4508-3

Legal deposit: 2nd trimester 2014
Bibliothèque et Archives nationales du Québec
National Library of Canada

Printed in Canada

2   3   4   5   6   ITIB   21   20   19   18   17

This project is funded in part by the Government of Canada

Canada

Acknowledgements

I wish to express deep gratitude to my dedicated editor, Melissa Repas, who encouraged, supported, and oversaw every detail of this project.

I would also like to thank the editorial team at Chenelière Education for their dedication, creativity, and attention to detail.

I am grateful to the helpful feedback of my colleagues across the province.

I would like to dedicate this book to my loving husband whose support and encouragement contributed greatly to the success of this project, as well as to my two sons, Joel and Lucas, who got me away from the computer for fun and family time, and to my wonderful mother whose advice, insight, and unconditional love help guide me through life.

– Sandra Cole

Thank you to the many teachers who gave invaluable feedback and suggestions, including the team of reviewers:
Rachel Benjamin, Cégep de St-Laurent
Jason Brunwald, Cégep de Lévis
Susan Frame, Cégep Marie-Victorin
Lucie Riopel, Cégep de Ste-Foy

And to those who participated in the developmental research for this second edition:
Vanessa Beal, Cégep Edouard-Montpetit
Jany Couture, Cégep Marie-Victorin
Charles Lapointe, Cégep de Ste-Foy
Jacinthe Paillé Landry, Collège André-Grasset
Carol Riera, Cégep de La Pocatière

Table of Contents

WRITING FILES 2 — The Essay

UNIT 4 — RELATIONSHIPS — Does Love Make the World Go Around?

UNIT 5 — STEREOTYPES — What's Your Impression?

WRITING FILES 3 — Improving Your Essay

Scope and Sequence

	READING	LISTENING / WATCHING	WRITING	SPEAKING
UNIT 1 Technology	• Skim a news article for main ideas • Scan a news article for specific information • Find and restate the main idea of a newspaper opinion piece	• Watch a news report for main ideas and details • Watch a documentary and take notes • Listen for vocabulary	• Write a short paragraph • Write a short dialogue using idiomatic expressions	• Ask questions in simple present • Make introductions • Describe your time-consuming technological habits to a small group • Role-play a dialogue using idioms • Talk about how you communicate

WRITING FILES 1 The Paragraph • Model paragraph • Generating ideas • Topic sentences • Supporting ideas • Revising and editing

	READING	LISTENING / WATCHING	WRITING	SPEAKING
UNIT 2 Personality	• Read and summarize an opinion poll • Use inference skills to understand a novel excerpt • Read a scientific magazine article for main ideas and details	• Watch a documentary for main ideas and details • Listen to a radio interview for main ideas and details • Use listening strategies to improve comprehension	• Write two paragraphs about your family history • Write a journal entry	• Agree and disagree with an opinion poll • Use the simple past to talk about your family origins • Discuss birth order
UNIT 3 Travel	• Read a piece of creative non-fiction to get meaning from context • Read a magazine article to exchange information	• Watch a short film for main ideas and details • Watch a documentary for main ideas and details	• Focus on descriptive writing • Write an adventure story	• Interview a classmate about his or her travel style • Discuss adventure travel, important life lessons and the culture of sharing • Role-play a dialogue using idioms • Paraphrase travel quotes

WRITING FILES 2 The Essay • Model essay • The thesis statement • The difference between a thesis statement and a topic sentence

	READING	LISTENING / WATCHING	WRITING	SPEAKING
UNIT 4 Relationships	• Activate prior knowledge • Read a magazine article • Team read and retell • Predict • Take notes on main ideas • Read and analyze a short story	• Watch a documentary for main ideas and details • Watch a photo-documentary and take notes	• Summarize data gathered during a survey interview • Write an essay	• Interview classmates • Conduct an opinion poll • Give your opinion using *should* • Discuss relationship types • Discuss a quote and the portrayal of love in other cultures
UNIT 5 Stereotypes	• Do timed readings • Summarize a reading • Read a magazine article for main ideas and details • Scan for specific vocabulary • Pair read and retell	• Watch a television news report for main ideas and details • Listen to a radio documentary for main ideas and details	• Write an opinion essay	• Discuss and explain reasons for first impressions • Describe a memory • Use expressions to formulate assumptions • Debate gender assumptions • Use debating language

WRITING FILES 3 Improving Your Essay • The introduction • Transition words • The conclusion • Revising for unity and cohesion

	READING	LISTENING / WATCHING	WRITING	SPEAKING
UNIT 6 Happiness	• Pair read and retell • Read for main ideas and details • Read a blog entry • Annotate a text	• Watch an informal documentary for main ideas and details • Watch a television news report for main ideas and details	• Write an argumentative essay	• Survey classmates to learn about money habits • Debate whether money can or can't buy happiness • Express yourself politely using modals
UNIT 7 Marketing	• Activate prior knowledge • Predict • Read for main ideas and details • Read an article and take notes	• Watch a documentary for main ideas and details • Listen for vocabulary • Listen to a radio show and take notes	• Write an argumentative essay • Write a summary	• Role-play a dialogue • Present a commercial at a focus group meeting • Think critically with a partner

WRITING FILES 4 Vocabulary and Word Choice • Informal versus standard English • False cognates • Commonly confused words

PRONUNCIATION	VOCABULARY	GRAMMAR	TOPIC FILES and PROJECTS (i+)
• Third-person singular -s	• Words, expressions, and idioms related to technology, communication, and time-consuming technological habits • Define words in a text using context clues	• Simple present • Frequency adverbs • Phrasal verbs • Present progressive	• Write a text or give an oral presentation on a topic related to technology (cellphones, video gaming, my generation, Facebook) • Conduct a survey
• The -ed ending of regular verbs in the simple past	• Words, expressions, and idioms related to family • Define words in a text using context	• Simple past • Past progressive	• Write a text or give an oral presentation on a topic related to personality (generation net, aboriginal culture, birth order, family history, nature vs. nurture) • Prepare a round-table presentation on a coming-of-age book or movie
• The /th/ sound	• Words, expressions, and idioms related to travel • Define words in a text using context	• Future	• Write a text or give an oral presentation on a topic related to travel (travel on the edge, volunteer travel, couchsurfing, the culture of sharing, travel lessons) • Create a travel show

• The essay outline • Revising and editing

PRONUNCIATION	VOCABULARY	GRAMMAR	TOPIC FILES and PROJECTS
• Word stress	• Words, expressions, and idioms related to relationships • Descriptive adjectives	• Question formation • Present perfect • Simple past • Adjectives • Mixed verb tenses	• Write a text or give an oral presentation on a topic related to relationships (the science of attraction, virtual love, relationship personality, arranged marriages, relationship mistakes) • Love across the generations survey
• The /h/ sound	• Words, expressions, and idioms related to impressions and biases • Use synonyms to define words • Debating language	• Comparatives and superlatives • Phrasal verbs	• Write a text or give an oral presentation on a topic related to stereotypes (first impressions, unconscious bias, the Human Library, beauty bias, gender differences) • Present and analyze stereotypes in music
• Can versus can't	• Words, expressions, and idioms related to money and happiness • Define or find synonyms of words in a text using context	• Modals	• Write a text or give an oral presentation on a topic related to happiness (money and happiness, one-week jobs, happy countries, laughology, party animals) • Test a happiness theory
• Cardinal and ordinal numbers	• Words, expressions, and idioms related to marketing	• Conditionals	• Write a text or give an oral presentation on a topic related to marketing (marketing to millennials, coolhunting, cause marketing, colours in marketing, hyper-target marketing) • Raise awareness about manipulative marketing campaigns

• The Academic Word List • Use a thesaurus

Features

In this second edition of *REAL Skills Book 2* you'll find the many features that made the first edition such a success along with valuable improvements and additions. The magazine-style integrated approach has been updated to suit the language needs of today's intermediate student. New and updated themes offering student-centred activities explore relevant issues and topics.

Overall Structure

Seven theme-based units are designed to pique your interest while building your language skills. There are also four step-by-step Writing Files to help you write effective paragraphs and essays. They have been regrouped to offer one period of class time. The book concludes with useful appendices to help you with your written and oral assignments.

Skills

Reading, Listening and Watching

Level-appropriate texts, videos, and audio material have been updated and come from a variety of authentic sources.

You will read a large selection of text types, including an excerpt from a short story and a novel, listen to interviews and reports, and watch high-interest documentaries and short films.

New targeted reading practice

Reading for Strategy allows you to practise a specific reading strategy to improve your reading skills.

Reading for Interaction encourages pair reading or structured discussion in class.

FYI (For Your Information) provides interesting facts or tips related to the theme.

Reading for Challenge offers you a more challenging or longer text.

New targeted grammar focus

Focus on Language is a new section that gives you the opportunity to focus on specific aspects of grammar that you see or hear in context.

Speaking and Writing

Engaging **warm-up** activities, such as surveys, quizzes, and interview scenarios, open each unit to get you thinking about and discussing the new theme.

Speaking activities offer **real contexts** and range from guided discussions and topical debates to creative role plays to formal presentations.

Numerous **writing** and **discussion** boxes throughout the unit give you opportunities to react to various topics.

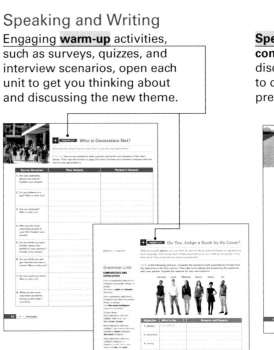

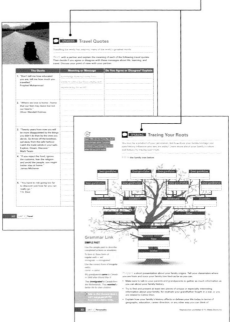

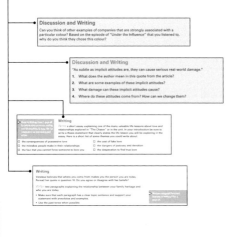

Topic Files

The new **Topic Files** section concludes each unit. It offers accessible writing and oral presentation topics to encourage you to explore the theme further. These activities reinforce the unit's featured language elements, which are listed in **Make the Connection**.

Top Words lists high-frequency vocabulary featured in the unit to help you to focus on these words and integrate them in your own speaking and writing.

Writing Files

Newly expanded, each of the four **Writing Files** takes you **step-by-step** through the writing process, and provides models, examples, and hands-on practice of the writing theory, **including revising and editing exercises**.

The grey pages of these sections are easy to find so they can be **referenced** at any time.

Language Elements

Grammar Link gives you language and grammar tools to help you do the required tasks.

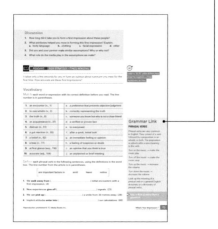

How To focuses on useful reading, listening, speaking, and writing strategies and now offers more explanations, examples, and concrete practice.

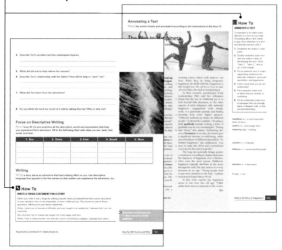

Pronunciation targets common difficulties and helps you become a more fluent speaker through guided practice.

The online pronunciation exercises provide automatic feedback.

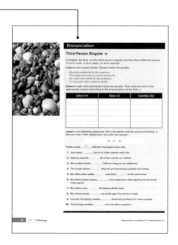

A variety of exercises helps you acquire new **vocabulary** carefully selected according to **frequency** and **usefulness**.

A section on **Idioms** helps you learn common theme-related expressions and put them into practice.

Cross-references indicate where to find more detailed information or practice.

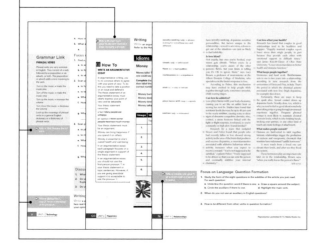

 Clear and integrated **web links** indicate when to consult the interactive activities online.

 Interactive **THE POWER OF AN EXCEPTIONAL DIGITAL TOOL**

- An interactive eBook for teachers and students
- Additional questions on material in the book and on new material found only online
- Immediate feedback to help better assess understanding and to monitor progress
- Creation and customization of interactive online activities by teachers
- Vocabulary exercises and quizzes to improve vocabulary use and retention
- Pronunciation workshops for online practice
- Access to the CD and DVD content that can be played directly from the platform
- Teacher tools such as projects, transcripts, answer keys, evaluation material, and grids

TECHNOLOGY

Are You a Digital Slave?

How communication is changing in a technological world

> How are texting, social networking, and video games changing the way we relate to others?

> Are smartphones and surfing the Internet making us more intelligent?

> How can video gamers save the world?

In this unit, you will learn more about the impact of your favourite technologies on your life.

ARE YOU HOOKED?

FYI

Judith Wright, author of *The Soft Addiction Solution*, describes soft addictions as "seemingly harmless habits like over-shopping, overeating, watching too much TV, endlessly surfing the Internet, and procrastinating that actually keep us from the life we want."

Grammar Link

SIMPLE PRESENT

Use the simple present to talk about permanent situations in the present, such as habitual actions, habits, and facts.

Pay attention to the position of adverbs of frequency. They usually go before the verb.
*I **often** answer my phone in class. I **never** send text messages in class.*

To form questions, use the auxiliary *do* or *does* and follow this formula:

QASVO (Question word + Auxiliary [*do* or *does*] + Subject + Verb + Object)
*How often **do** you watch TV?*
*How many hours **does** he spend downloading music?*

▶ Refer to *REAL Grammar Book 2,* unit 1.

💬 How To

MAKE INTRODUCTIONS

Use the following expressions:

I'd like you to meet Julie.

Let me introduce you to David.

I would like to introduce you to Marie.

 **WARM-UP** # How Do You Spend Your Time?

Are your harmless habits—gaming, surfing, and texting—taking up a lot of your time? Be careful! These activities can become soft addictions when you do them too often.

Interview a classmate to find out how often he or she uses technology. Write a question in the simple present to ask your partner. Make sure to use the question words *how often*. Answer the question with one of the frequency adverbs in the following box.

| Always | Frequently | Often | Sometimes | Occasionally | Rarely | Never |

Activity	Question	Partner's Answer
1. Answer cellphone in class	How often do you answer your cellphone in class?	
2. Send text messages		
3. Download music or movies		
4. Watch TV		
5. Use social media		
6. Play video games		
7. Download new apps		
8. Other:		

Introduce a partner to another pair of students. Describe your partner's favourite time-consuming activity. Remember to add *-s* to the third-person singular verbs that describe your partner's activities.

Let me introduce you to Maxime. He often plays video games and he checks Facebook at least five times a day.

Writing

Write a short paragraph about your partner's favourite time-consuming activity. Underline all the present tense verbs that end with *-s*.

Can video games teach us valuable life lessons? Jane McGonigal, game developer and author of *Reality is Broken: Why Games Make Us Better and How They Can Change the World*, says yes!

Vocabulary

Match each word or expression with its definition before you read. The line number is in parentheses.

1.	a misconception (n., 1)	**a.**	to accomplish
2.	escapist (adj., 2)	**b.**	a reality
3.	a waste of time (exp., 2)	**c.**	helping to avoid reality
4.	to spend time (exp., 6)	**d.**	a recompense
5.	pride (n., 31)	**e.**	a wrong idea
6.	to achieve (v., 32)	**f.**	to use time
7.	a truth (n., 41)	**g.**	an unproductive use of time
8.	a reward (n., 46)	**h.**	self-esteem

Skimming and Scanning

Skim the article on page 4 and highlight the first line of every paragraph. Remember that skimming is done quickly.

1. Put a check mark next to the themes discussed in the article.

☐ **a.** Playing video games is a productive way to spend time.

☐ **b.** Video games teach us real-world skills.

☐ **c.** Gamers should spend more time in the real world.

☐ **d.** Video games are bad for our health.

☐ **e.** Video gamers are more creative and optimistic.

☐ **f.** Video games make us more intelligent.

Scan the text and find this information:

2. Percentage of boys under 18 who game: _____

3. Percentage of girls under 18 who game: _____

4. The number of hours gamers accumulate before the age of 21: _____

5. The title of the book mentioned in the article: _____

6. The names of two video games mentioned: _____

 How To

SKIM AND SCAN

Skimming is a useful way to get a general idea of a text before you read it.

- Move your eyes quickly through the whole text, reading the title and the first line of every paragraph.
- Look briefly at the illustrations or photos.
- Don't stop for details or to look up unfamiliar words in a dictionary.

Scanning is a useful way to read for specific facts and details. We all practise the technique of scanning when we look up a word in a dictionary.

- Move your eyes quickly over the text until you find the specific piece of information you are looking for.

Video Games: An Hour a Day Is Key to Success in Life

By Jane McGonigal

The single biggest misconception about games is that they're an escapist waste of time. But more than a decade's worth of scientific research shows that gaming is actually one of the most productive ways we can spend time. Games help us produce something more important than the **economic bottom line**: powerful emotions and social relationships that can change our lives. They can also help us change the world.

Currently there are more than half a billion people worldwide playing online games for at least an hour a day. The younger you are, the more likely you are to be a gamer: 97% of boys under 18 and 94% of girls under 18 report playing video games regularly. The average young person racks up 10 000 hours of gaming by the age of 21. That's almost exactly as much time as they spend in a classroom during all of **middle school** and high school if they have perfect **attendance**. Most astonishingly, five million gamers in the United States are spending more than 40 hours a week playing games—the same as a full-time job!

Why are we increasingly turning to games? According to my research, it's because games do a better job than ordinary life of provoking our most powerful positive emotions, like curiosity, optimism, pride, and a desire to join forces with others to achieve something extraordinary. Games also, increasingly, are a particularly effective way to **bond** with our friends and family. That's what I mean when I say—in the title of my new book—that "Reality is Broken." The fact that so many people of all ages, all over the world, are choosing to spend so much time in game worlds is a sign of something important, a truth that we urgently need to recognize.

The truth is this: In today's society, computer and video games are fulfilling genuine human needs that the real world is currently unable to satisfy. Games are providing rewards that reality is not. They are teaching and inspiring and engaging us in ways that reality is not. They are bringing us together in ways that reality is not. And unless something dramatic happens to reverse the resulting **exodus**, we're fast on our way to becoming a society in which a substantial portion of our population devotes its greatest efforts to playing games, creates its best memories in game environments, and experiences its biggest successes in game worlds. Fortunately, however, this temporary exodus is not a complete waste of time!

When we play a good game, we become more optimistic, more creative, more focused, more likely to set ambitious goals, and more resilient in the face of **failure**. When we play multiplayer games, we become more collaborative and more likely to help others. More importantly, playing a game with someone is an incredibly effective way to get to know their **strengths** and **weaknesses**— as well as what motivates them. This is exactly the kind of social knowledge we need to be able to cooperate and collaborate with people to **tackle** real-world challenges.

The good news about games is that recent scientific research shows that all of these feelings and activities can **trickle** into our real lives. For example, kids who spend just 30 minutes playing a "pro-social" game like *Super Mario Sunshine* (in which players clean up pollution and graffiti around an island) are more likely to help others in real life for a full week after playing the game. People of all ages who play musical games like *Rock Band* and *Guitar Hero* report spending more time learning and playing real musical instruments than before they started playing the video game. Just 90 seconds of playing a game like *World of Warcraft*—where you have a powerful avatar—can boost the confidence of college students so much that for up to 24 hours later, they're more likely to be successful taking a test at school . . . and to be more **outgoing** in real-world social situations.

This "spill-over" effect of games means that young people who identify strongly as

>>

economic bottom line (exp.) → net income or loss

exodus (n.) → departure of many people

failure (n.) → lack of success

middle school (n.) → a school between elementary and high school, usually for grades six to eight

attendance (n.) → presence in class

strengths (n.) → best qualities

weaknesses (n.) → worst qualities

tackle (v.) → attempt to solve

trickle (v.) → move slowly

bond (v.) → connect psychologically

outgoing (adj.) → extroverted

Read "Video Game Addiction: Does It Exist?" online for a contrasting viewpoint.

gamers have real-world talents and strengths that will undoubtedly serve them well in the future, if they understand that these are real skills and abilities, not just virtual ones. That's why I wanted to write *Reality is Broken*: to show gamers (and parents of gamers) exactly how playing games can prepare us to tackle challenges like curing cancer, ending world hunger, and stopping climate change. (Yes, it's true! There are games to help players do all of these things.)

Of course, there can always be too much of a good thing. Studies show that playing games for up to 21 hours a week can have a positive impact on your health and happiness, especially if you're playing games face to face with friends and family, or playing cooperative games (rather than competitive games). That's why I recommend that parents of gamers spend as much time as possible playing, too. In fact, a new study revealed that daughters who play video games with their parents report feeling much closer to their parents and demonstrate significantly lower levels of aggression, behaviour problems, and depression.

However, when you hit 28 hours a week of gaming or more, it starts to distract you from real-life goals and other kinds of social interaction that are essential to leading a good life. Multiple studies have shown that with more than three hours a day, you're not going to get those positive impacts. Instead, you'll be at risk for negative impacts like depression and social anxiety.

So what's the optimal level of gaming? For most people, an hour a day playing our favourite games will power up our ability to engage wholeheartedly with difficult challenges, strengthen our relationships with the people we care about most (while still letting us notice when it's time to stop playing in virtual worlds), and bring our gamer strengths back to real life.

988 words

Comprehension

Read the entire article and answer the following questions.

1. Why are people spending more and more time playing video games?

2. What kind of social knowledge about others do video games help us develop?

3. How can playing certain games have positive effects in the real world? Complete the chart.

Game	Time Spent	Positive Result in the Real World
a. *Super Mario Sunshine*		
b. *Rock Band / Guitar Hero*	—	
c. *World of Warcraft*		

4. How many hours of video gaming a week are too many? _____

5. What are two negative effects of too much gaming?

a. _____ **b.** _____

Focus on Language: Phrasal Verbs and the Present Tenses

1. Find a phrasal verb in the paragraph indicated that means the following:

a. to accumulate (2): _____

b. to focus our attention on (3): _____

c. to start (10): _____

2. Scan paragraph four. Find the following verbs and write the conjugated form.

a. to fulfill: _____ **b.** to provide: _____

c. to teach: _____ **d.** to bring: _____

e. What verb tense is this? _____

f. How is it formed?

_____

g. Why is this verb tense used in this paragraph?

_____

3. Scan paragraph five. Find the following verbs and write the conjugated form.

a. to play: _____ **b.** to become: _____

c. to motivate _____ **d.** to need: _____

e. What verb tense is this? _____

f. How is it formed?

_____

g. Why is this verb tense used in this paragraph?

_____

Grammar Link

PHRASAL VERBS

Phrasal verbs are very common in English. They consist of a verb followed by a preposition or an adverb, or both. The preposition or adverb adds a new meaning to the verb.

Turn on the music → make the music play

Turn off the music → make the music stop

Turn up the music → increase the volume

Turn down the music → decrease the volume

Look up the meanings of phrasal verbs in a general English dictionary or a dictionary of phrasal verbs.

➤ **Refer to** *REAL Grammar Book 2,* **appendix 6.**

➤ **Refer to Writing Files 1, page 21, for more information on the paragraph.**

Discussion

1. What video games do you play?

2. Do you ever feel that you are wasting your time when you play video games? Explain your answer.

3. Do you learn anything useful by playing these games? Explain your answer.

Writing

Write a paragraph on whether you agree with the author that gaming prepares us to face real-life challenges like finding a cure for cancer or ending world hunger. Explain your opinion in one paragraph.

⟨⟩ WATCHING Texting: Can We Pull the Plug?

These days, it seems like everyone has a cellphone that they can't live without. CBS News: *Sunday Morning* looks at the impact of this form of instant communication.

Discussion

1. How many text messages and calls do you receive on average every day?
2. Are you able to spend a day without your cellphone? Why or why not?
3. Do you think that cellphones are bringing us closer together or driving us apart?

Fill in the following chart with a partner before you watch the report.

Positive Aspects of Cellphones	Negative Aspects of Cellphones
It is easy for people to reach you.	They can be disruptive.

Vocabulary

Watch the introduction to the video and then fill in the blanks with the missing words. Then, write a synonym or short definition in parentheses for each missing word.

Once upon a time, in what seems a far-off land, if you saw someone walking down the street talking to himself,

you'd think he was, well, _____crazy_____ (_____insane_____). Not anymore. Ninety percent of American adults

_____[1] (_____) cellphones and, whether talking or _____[2]

(_____), it seems that 90 percent of the time, they are using them. These days, the

minute that people are _____[3] (_____) at a stop sign, at the checkout line in a supermarket,

they panic, they _____[4] (_____) a phone. Psychologist Sherry Turkle says _____[5]

(_____) connections have left us more _____[6] (_____) than ever.

Comprehension

Watch the rest of the video and answer the following questions.

1. Where does Sherry Turkle find people texting? Name three places.

_____

Listen to "This Is Your Brain Online" online to learn more about how the Internet is rewiring our brains.

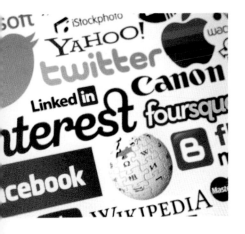

2. What conclusion does Sherry Turkle reach in her book *Alone Together*?

3. Are we addicted to our phones? What is Turkle's opinion?

4. What two accidents were caused by texting while walking?

   a. _____ b. _____

5. Researchers ask students around the world not to use their cellphones for 24 hours.

   a. How many of them quit the experiment? _____

   b. Why did they quit? _____

6. What scientific reason does Nicholas Carr give to explain our obsession with smartphones?

7. Why was the young child confused when she was playing with a magazine?

8. According to the interview, are smartphones bad for our brains?

Refer to the chart on page 7. Did you learn anything about smartphones that you want to add to the list?

 **SPEAKING** ## Time-Consuming Technologies

Is it video games, surfing, texting, Facebooking? We all have a time-wasting habit or two. What is yours?

Describe your most time-consuming digital habit to a small group of classmates. Use the simple present where possible. Use the following questions to guide your discussion.

• How many hours a day or week do you spend on this activity? Why?

• How do you feel when you are doing this activity?

• How do you react when someone suggests that you spend less time on this activity?

• Do you think you spend too much time doing this activity? Explain your answer.

• Do you plan to change your habits? Explain your answer.

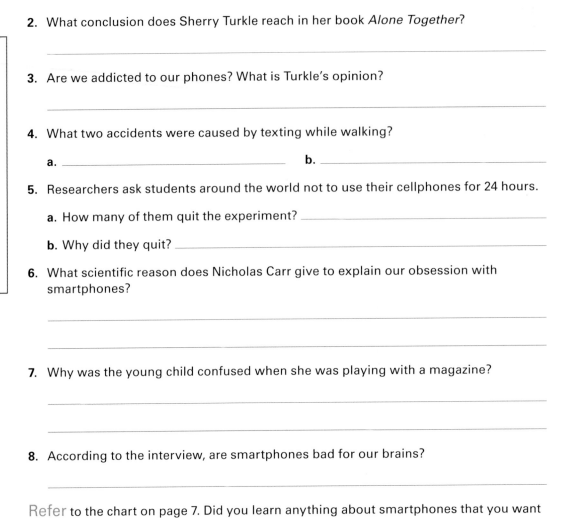

How is the Internet affecting our creativity, our intelligence, and our memories? Some scientists think that the Internet may be rewiring our brains. What do you think?

Discussion and Comprehension

Discuss with a partner how the Internet is affecting the way we accomplish certain activities. Write your thoughts in point form in the second column. Use the present progressive in your answers. Then read the article on page 10 and use information from it to fill in the final column.

Grammar Link

PRESENT PROGRESSIVE

Use the present progressive to describe temporary situations and actions in progress.

To form it:
Verb *be* + base form of the main verb + *-ing*

They **are** text**ing** each other.

▶ Refer to *REAL Grammar Book 2,* unit 1.

How is the Internet affecting the way we . . .	What You and Your Partner Think	What the Article Says
1. remember information?		
2. learn at school?		
3. concentrate?		
4. find information?		
5. read?		
6. spend time?		

Ten Big Ways the Internet Is Changing Our Brains

Adapted by OnlineCollege.org

We live in a world with the Internet, where nearly the entire wealth of human knowledge can live at our fingertips. Such an amazing feat, of course, doesn't happen without impacting our lives, and scientists have begun to
5 note that the Internet has not only served to fulfill our brains' curiosities, but has also rewired them. So what exactly is the Internet doing to our brains?

1. THE INTERNET IS OUR EXTERNAL HARD DRIVE We don't have to remember phone numbers or addresses anymore.
10 Instead, we can just hop on our email or Google to look them up. In a study by *Science* magazine, students were asked to type in pieces of trivia, and depending on their group were told that their information would be either erased or saved. The group that was told its data would be saved was less likely to
15 remember it. This study indicates that people have lower rates of recall when they can expect to be able to access information in the future.

2. CHILDREN ARE LEARNING DIFFERENTLY Remember all of the history lessons that required you to remember dates,
20 names, and finite details? Kids don't do that nearly as much as they used to. With online libraries, "rote memorization is no longer a necessary part of education." Educators are beginning to understand that memorizing facts wastes valuable brain power that could be used to keep up with more important information
25 that can't be quickly Googled.

3. WE HARDLY EVER GIVE TASKS OUR FULL ATTENTION Have you ever updated your Facebook while listening to music and texting a friend? If so, you've experienced the phenomenon of continuous partial attention and its impact on your brain. It
30 remains to be seen if partial attention is a distraction as most believe, or an adaptation of the brain to the constant flow of stimuli.

4. WE'RE GETTING BETTER AT FINDING INFORMATION Although we can't remember it all, we're getting better at
35 finding the information we need. It seems that the brainpower previously used to retain facts and information is now being used to remember how to look it up. Professor Betsy Sparrow reports, "We remember less through knowing information itself than by knowing where the information can be found." She indicates
40 that this isn't necessarily a bad thing, and may even be "kind of amazing," as we're adapting to new technology and becoming highly skilled at remembering where to find things.

5. DIFFICULT QUESTIONS MAKE US THINK ABOUT COMPUTERS When faced with a difficult question, people
45 rarely consider an encyclopedia or history books but, rather, think about computers. It's a brand-new impulse that exists in our brains. Because students in college often have to complete a lot of research, using the Internet has become all too common. For many, this means we don't have to trek to the library or, since
50 so many people have smartphones, even go much farther than our own pockets.

6. IQ IS INCREASING OVER TIME In the age of MTV and video games, parents and experts worried that the new and flashy technologies would fry our poor brains into oblivion. But
55 the exact opposite has happened: after MTV, after video games, after Twitter, Facebook, and Google, we're getting smarter. Are we smarter because of technology or in spite of it?

7. OUR CONCENTRATION IS SUFFERING In an article for the *Atlantic*, Nicholas Carr relates his growing difficulty in deep
60 reading. Like so many others, he finds that "deep reading that used to come naturally has become a struggle." It's not hard to figure out why. Our time online is often spent scanning headlines and posts and quickly surfing links, never spending much time on any one thing. So of course, when it comes to reading for
65 more than a few minutes, or even moments, your mind will often begin to wander.

8. WE'RE BECOMING PHYSICALLY ADDICTED TO TECHNOLOGY Even after unplugging, many Internet users feel a craving for the stimulation received from gadgets. The
70 culprit is dopamine, which is delivered as a response to the stimulation—without it, you feel bored. After spending time online, your brain wants to get back on for more, making it difficult to concentrate on other tasks and "unplug."

**9. OUR BRAINS CONSTANTLY SEEK OUT INCOMING
75 INFORMATION** Tests at Stanford University indicate that multitaskers, such as heavy Internet users, often tend to overlook older, valuable information, instead choosing to seek out new information. Instead of focusing on important tasks or putting information to good use, we're distracted by incoming email.

80 **10. ONLINE THINKING PERSISTS EVEN OFFLINE** When you're online, you're frequently attacked by bursts of information, which are highly stimulating and even overwhelming. Too much, and you can become extremely distracted and unfocused. Even after you log off (if you ever do), your brain remains rewired.
85 A lack of focus and fractured thinking can persist, interrupting work, family, and offline time.

810 words

<o> **WATCHING** Facebook Follies

Is Facebook fundamentally changing the way we communicate? In this documentary from *CBC Doc Zone*, you will learn more about the unexpected consequences of sharing our private lives so publicly.

Discussion

1. How many Facebook friends do you have? Do you know all of them personally?

2. What kind of information do you post on Facebook?

3. Have you ever posted a comment or a photo that you regret? Explain your answer.

Vocabulary

Match each word or expression with its definition before you watch.

1. to bring us closer (exp.)		**a.** to be more important or significant than
2. to share (v.)		**b.** to unite
3. racy (adj.)		**c.** to use together
4. to outweigh (v.)		**d.** old-fashioned
5. quaint (adj.)		**e.** slightly indecent, risqué
6. to show up (v.)		**f.** to resign from a position
7. to come to an end (exp.)		**g.** to stop or cease
8. to step down (exp.)		**h.** to attend

Watch the first part of the documentary and fill in the blanks with the words you hear.

9. This Doc Zone is all about Facebook _____ .

10. One of our basic needs is _____ with others.

11. All the innovations in communication served the same purpose: to bring people

    _____ together.

12. We record our lives, we interact with other, and we _____ our personal experiences online.

13. All this sharing comes with a personal _____ .

14. Social media are changing the way people _____ .

15. . . . with _____ down the road that are impossible to predict.

Note-Taking

Watch the second part of the documentary and take notes about each Facebook folly.

 **How To**

TAKE NOTES WHILE YOU LISTEN

Note-taking helps you understand and remember what you hear.

• Listen carefully and write down the main ideas in your own words.

• Don't try to write down everything the speaker says, or try to write word-for-word notes.

Event	Person Give, for example, name, age, nationality, employment.	Folly Describe what happened.	Consequences Describe the repercussions.
1. The birthday party	16-year-old Thessa from Germany		
2. The election			

3. Who is Clive Thompson? What is his area of expertise? What does he say?

Event			
4. The royal wedding			

5. What does this documentary say about the future of Facebook?

Comprehension

Use your notes and answer the following questions.

1. Why did so many teenagers show up at Thessa's house?

_____

_____

_____

2. Where is Ray Lamb from? What political party did he run for?

_____

_____

3. How does Facebook make social forgetting more difficult?

_____

_____

_____

4. What was the name of Cameron Reilly's regiment? How would you describe his future in the military?

_____

_____

_____

5. Explain what this statement means: "Facebook will be as quaint as the telegraph."

_____

_____

_____

Discussion and Writing

1. How do you think Facebook will change us as a society?

2. How do you think Facebook itself will change and evolve?

Pronunciation

Third-Person Singular -s

In English, the final -s of the third-person singular can have three different sounds: /s/ as in *surfs*, /z/ as in *plays*, /iz/ as in *watches*.

Listen to the tongue twister. Repeat it after the speaker.

She sells seashells by the seashore.
The shells she sells are surely seashells.
So if she sells shells on the seashore,
I'm sure she sells seashore shells.

Listen to each verb and repeat it after the speaker. Then write the verb in the appropriate column according to the pronunciation of the final -s.

Likes /s/	Sees /z/	Catches /iz/

Listen to the following sentences. Fill in the blanks with the sound of the final -s that you hear. Then repeat each verb after the speaker.

/s/   /z/   /iz/

Phillip sends ___/z/___ 300 text messages every day.

1. Joel plays _____ hours of video games each day.

2. Sabrina spends _____ all of her money on clothes.

3. My mother thinks _____ I talk too long on my cellphone.

4. The study shows _____ that we are becoming isolated and lonely.

5. My little sister walks _____ and texts _____ at the same time.

6. My little brother seems _____ more optimistic after playing his favourite video game.

7. My father uses _____ his laptop all the time.

8. My friend works _____ out at the gym five times a week.

9. Impulse shopping creates _____ financial problems for many people.

10. Technology enables _____ us to be alone together.

Communication

No matter how you choose to communicate with your world—face to face or via a virtual interface—you will encounter and use many idiomatic expressions in English.

Match each idiom with its meaning. Write the correct letter in the second column. In the third column, write a sentence using the idiomatic expression.

Idiomatic Expression	Meaning	Sentence
1. to drop someone a line	c	I will drop you a line tonight so we can finalize our plans for the weekend.
2. to get it straight from the horse's mouth		
3. to get our wires crossed		
4. to get straight to the point		
5. to hear it through the grapevine		
6. to see eye to eye		
7. to speak of the devil		
8. to stay in touch		
9. to take what someone says with a grain of salt		
10. to talk someone's ear off		

Meaning

a. to have a misunderstanding
b. to hear news from an unofficial source
c. to communicate with someone in writing
d. to talk for a very long time
e. to agree with someone
f. to hear news from an authoritative source

g. said when a person appears just after being mentioned
h. to maintain communication with someone
i. to focus on the most important thing without delay
j. to believe only part of what someone says

FYI

Did you know there are over 25 000 idioms in the English language? Idioms are words or expressions that cannot be taken literally. For example, if someone tells you to "break a leg" before a job interview, they are wishing you good luck.

Writing

Work with a partner and write a short conversation between two friends. Use at least three of the idiomatic expressions. Then act out your dialogue for another group of students. Can you understand the idioms they use?

SPEAKING | Say What?

When you think of communicating with someone, do you automatically turn to your smartphone or does it depend on the person and the situation?

Fill in the second column of the chart with your preferred method of communication for each situation. Then discuss with a partner and write their answers in the third column. Choose from the following methods of communication.

call cellphone	place video call	send instant message
call home phone	post online publicly	send text message
face-to-face	send email	other: _____

The Situation	How You Choose to Communicate	How Your Partner Chooses to Communicate
1. To tell your parents you will be late for supper	I send my mom a text message.	She calls her dad on his cellphone.
2. To break up with your boyfriend or girlfriend		
3. To wish your brother or sister a happy birthday		
4. To tell someone about your bad day		
5. To meet your friends at a party		
6. To organize a high school reunion		
7. To do homework or work on a project with someone		
8. To offer someone condolences		

Discussion

1. Based on your answers in the chart, what is the most popular method of communication? What is the least popular method of communication? What do your answers say about you and your generation?

2. How is technology changing the way we communicate with others? Explain your answer.

In an article from the *New York Times*, Sherry Turkle challenges us to take a hard look at the changes texting and social media are making to our lives.

Vocabulary

Write a short definition of each of the following words. The line number is in parentheses. Use context clues or your dictionary to help you.

1. flight (n., 0)	
2. plugged-in (adj., 16)	
3. fearing (adj., 29)	
4. to shortchange (v., 48)	
5. caring (n., 50)	
6. to dumb down (v., 78)	
7. appealing (adj., 84)	
8. to flee (v., 111)	

The Flight from Conversation
By Sherry Turkle
New York Times

We live in a technological universe in which we are always communicating. And yet we have sacrificed conversation for mere connection.

5 At home, families sit together, texting and reading email. At work, executives text during board meetings. We text (and shop and go on Facebook) during classes and when we're on dates. My students tell me about an 10 important new skill. It involves maintaining eye contact with someone while you text someone else. It's hard, but it can be done.

Over the past 15 years, I've studied technologies of mobile connection and 15 talked to hundreds of people of all ages and circumstances about their plugged-in lives. I've learned that the little devices most of us carry around are so powerful that they change not only what we do, but also who we are.

20 We've become accustomed to a new way of being "alone together." Technology-enabled, we are able to be with one another, and also elsewhere, connected to wherever we want to be. We want to customize our lives. We want to 25 move in and out of where we are because the thing we value most is control over where we focus our attention.

In today's workplace, young people who have grown up fearing conversation show 30 up on the job wearing earphones. Walking through a college library or the campus of a high-tech start-up, one sees the same thing: we are together, but each of us is in our own bubble, furiously connected to keyboards 35 and tiny touch screens.

In the silence of connection, people are comforted by being in touch with a lot of people—carefully kept at bay. We can't get enough of one another if we can use 40 technology to keep one another at distances we can control: not too close, not too far, just right.

>>

Human relationships are rich; they're complicated and demanding. We have
45 learned the habit of cleaning them up with technology. And the move from conversation to connection is part of this. But it's a process in which we shortchange ourselves. Worse, it seems that over time
50 we stop caring, we forget that there is a difference.

We are tempted to think that our little "**sips**" of online connection add up to a big **gulp** of real conversation. But they
55 don't. Email, Twitter, Facebook, all of these have their places—in politics, commerce, romance, and friendship. But no matter how valuable, they are not a substitute for conversation.

60 Connecting in sips may work for gathering small separate bits of information or for saying, "I am thinking about you." Or even for saying, "I love you." But connecting in sips doesn't work
65 as well when it comes to understanding and knowing one another. In conversation we **tend** to one another. We can attend to tone and nuance. In conversation, we are called upon to see things from another's
70 point of view.

Face-to-face conversation unfolds slowly. It teaches patience. When we communicate on our digital devices, we learn different habits. As we **ramp up** the
75 volume and velocity of online connections, we start to expect faster answers. To get these, we ask one another simpler questions; we dumb down our communications.

During the years I have spent
80 researching people and their relationships with technology, I have often heard the sentiment "No one is listening to me." I believe this feeling helps explain why it is so appealing to have a Facebook page or
85 a Twitter feed—each provides so many automatic listeners. And it helps explain why—against all reason—so many of us are willing to talk to machines that seem to care about us.

90 We expect more from technology and less from one another and seem increasingly drawn to technologies that provide the illusion of companionship without the demands of relationship.
95 Always-on/always-on-you devices provide three powerful fantasies: that we will always be heard; that we can put our attention wherever we want it to be; and that we never have to be alone. Indeed our
100 new devices have turned being alone into a problem that can be solved.

Think of it as "I share, therefore I am." We use technology to define ourselves by sharing our thoughts and feelings as we're
105 having them. We used to think, "I have a feeling; I want to make a call." Now our impulse is, "I want to have a feeling; I need to send a text."

So, in order to feel more, and to feel more
110 like ourselves, we connect. But in our rush to connect, we flee from solitude, our ability to be separate and gather ourselves. Lacking the capacity for solitude, we turn to other people but don't experience them as they
115 are. It is as though we use them, need them as spare parts to support our increasingly fragile selves. We think constant connection will make us feel less lonely. The opposite is true. If we are unable to be alone, we are far
120 more likely to be lonely.

I am a partisan for conversation. To make room for it, I see some first, deliberate steps. At home, we can create sacred spaces: the kitchen, the dining room. We can make
125 our cars "device-free zones." And we can do the same thing at work. There we are so busy communicating that we often don't have time to talk to one another about what really matters. Most of all, we need
130 to remember—in between texts and emails and Facebook posts—to listen to one another, even to the boring bits, because it is often in unedited moments, moments in which we hesitate and stutter and go silent,
135 that we reveal ourselves to one another.

Not too long ago, people walked with their heads up, looking at the water, the sky, the sand and at one another, talking. Now they often walk with their heads down,
140 typing. Even when they are with friends, partners, children, everyone is on their own devices. So I say, look up, look at one another and let's start the conversation.

Sherry Turkle is a psychologist and *professor at M.I.T. and the author of* Alone Together: Why We Expect More from Technology and Less from Each Other.

145

999 words

sips (n.) → small mouthfuls of a drink

gulp (n.) → large mouthful of a drink

tend (v.) → pay attention

ramp up (v.) → increase

Comprehension

1. Scan the article for the main idea. Describe it in one sentence.

   _____

   _____

2. What does it mean to be "alone together"? Give an example from the text.

   _____

   _____

3. When does connecting in "sips" work? When does it not work?

   _____

   _____

4. How does face-to-face conversation teach patience?

   _____

5. What three powerful fantasies do virtual communication devices offer us?

   a. _____

   b. _____

   c. _____

6. How has our use of technology changed the way we define ourselves? Use your own words to explain.

   _____

   _____

   _____

7. How does constant connection make us feel lonely?

   _____

   _____

8. How can we make room for more conversation in our lives?

   _____

   _____

   _____

9. Why should we make room for more conversation in our lives?

   _____

   _____

FIND THE MAIN IDEA

The main idea is the point a writer makes about a topic.

To find the main idea:

1. Define the general topic of the text.

2. Ask yourself what point the writer makes about the topic.

3. Write the topic of the text and the author's opinion in one or two sentences.

Write a text or give an oral presentation clearly explaining your opinion on one of the statements below. Try to incorporate the elements seen in the unit from the Make the Connection box and use as many of the Top Words as you can, where appropriate.

Agree or disagree with one of these statements:

1 MY CELLPHONE use has a negative impact on my personal relationships.

2 VIDEO GAMING is an escapist waste of time.

3 SURFING the Internet is making me smarter.

4 VIDEO GAMING is preparing my generation to confront and find solutions to real-world problems.

5 MY GENERATION is losing the art of face-to-face communication.

6 FACEBOOK is changing our society.

7 OTHER: _____ Write about another topic of your choice linked to what you learned in this unit. Make sure you have your topic approved by your teacher.

Make the Connection

- [ ] Simple present and present progressive
- [ ] Phrasal verbs
- [ ] Vocabulary and idioms from the unit
- [ ] Pronouncing the third-person singular -s
- [ ] Skimming and scanning
- [ ] Finding the main idea
- [ ] Making introductions
- [ ] Writing coherent paragraphs and topic sentences

▶ Refer to Writing Files 1, page 21, for more about paragraphs.

▶ Refer to appendix 1, page 155, for more about oral presentations.

Vocabulary from the unit and other theme-related vocabulary can be practised online.

Top Words

Put a check mark next to the words you know and refer to the page numbers in the unit to learn the ones you don't know. Add to the list other words you want to remember from the unit.

ADJECTIVES
- [ ] alone (7)
- [ ] appealing (17)
- [ ] disconnected (7)
- [ ] escapist (2)
- [ ] plugged-in (17)

NOUNS
- [ ] a misconception (2)
- [ ] pride (2)
- [ ] a reward (2)
- [ ] a risk (11)
- [ ] a truth (2)

VERBS
- [ ] to achieve (2)
- [ ] to fear (17)
- [ ] to flee (17)
- [ ] to outweigh (11)
- [ ] to reach for (7)
- [ ] to share (11)

EXPRESSIONS
- [ ] to bring us closer (11)
- [ ] to come to an end (11)
- [ ] to dumb down (17)
- [ ] a waste of time (2)

OTHER:

_____ _____

_____ _____

_____ _____

The Paragraph

Model Paragraph

A paragraph is a collection of related sentences dealing with a single topic. To be effective, a paragraph must contain the following elements.

A clear topic sentence that states the main idea of the paragraph

When we play a good video game, we get to practise being the best version of ourselves. We become more optimistic, more creative, more focused, more likely to set ambitious goals, and more resilient in the face of failure. When we play multiplayer games, we become more collaborative and more likely to help others. In fact, we like and trust each other more after we play a game together, even if we lose. More importantly, playing a game with someone is an incredibly effective way to get to know their strengths and weaknesses, as well as what motivates them. This is exactly the kind of social knowledge we need to be able to cooperate and collaborate with people to tackle real-world challenges.

Supporting sentences that prove, illustrate, or explain the topic sentence

A concluding sentence that restates the main idea, reinforces the main point, and provides a link to the next paragraph

Generating Ideas

The first step in the writing process is to choose a topic, narrow it down, personalize it, and decide what you want to say about it. At the prewriting stage, there are three important questions that you have to answer:

1. What do I want to write about? (Choose a subject that you know about and are interested in.)

2. Who do I want to write to or for? (Choose an audience.)

3. Why do I want to write about this? (Decide on your purpose.)

Now that you have your subject, audience, and purpose for writing, you need to come up with your thoughts, feelings, and ideas about the topic. The most common techniques used to generate ideas are **brainstorming**, **freewriting**, **questioning**, and **cluster-mapping**.

Choose one of the topics from the box and generate as many ideas as you can. Use two different techniques. Write your ideas in the space provided. Which technique helps you generate the most ideas?

communication
education
generation net
siblings
social media
video games
other: _____

TOPIC: _____

TECHNIQUE

BRAINSTORMING is an effective way to think of new ideas alone or in small groups. To brainstorm, say or write in point form every idea about a given subject that comes to mind. Do not worry about spelling or structure at this stage.

- _____
- _____
- _____

FREEWRITING allows you to write freely, in sentences, all your ideas on a given subject without worrying about errors, organization, or word choice. To freewrite effectively, set a time limit and write all of the ideas that come to mind as quickly as you can.

_____
_____
_____
_____

QUESTIONING allows you to explore your subject by asking questions. Each question is a probe that allows you to see below the surface to find out what you already know about the subject and what you would like to find out.

Who _____   Why _____
What _____   How _____
Where _____   How often _____
When _____   How much _____

CLUSTER-MAPPING allows you to map your ideas visually and to create associations between your thoughts. The word *cluster* means a group of similar things. To create a cluster map, write the topic in the centre of the map and then write general ideas about the topic around it. Continue making associations between your ideas.

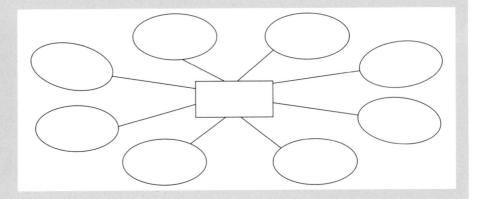

Topic Sentences

Once you have completed the prewriting step, you are ready to write a clear, well-organized paragraph. The first step is to craft an effective topic sentence. The topic sentence tells the reader what the paragraph is about.

- It introduces the topic of the paragraph.
- It includes a controlling idea that makes a point about the topic.
- It focuses the paragraph and makes a statement that is neither too broad nor too narrow.
- It is often the first sentence of the paragraph.

The first step in writing a topic sentence is to choose a topic and a general point of view or an idea about it.

Topic	Point of View
Gaming	is negative.

OR

Topic	Point of View
Gaming	is positive.

The next step is to narrow down the topic by finding a focus for the paragraph, called the controlling idea. The controlling idea answers these questions:

- What do I want to say about my topic?
- What specific point do I want to make about my topic?

Topic + Controlling Idea =	Topic Sentence
Video games + waste of time	Video games are an escapist waste of time.

OR

Topic + Controlling Idea =	Topic Sentence
Video games + real-life skills	Video games teach real-life skills.

Practice 1

Put a check mark next to the correct topic sentences. Explain what is wrong with the incorrect topic sentences and revise them to make them more effective.

❗ Do not write "This paragraph is about" or "I'm going to write about."

1. ☐ I am going to explain my time-consuming habit.

_____

_____

2. ☐ Spending too many hours on social-media sites can cause people to feel isolated.

_____

_____

3. ☐ This paragraph is about video games and online shopping.

_____

_____

4. ☐ Many people around the world own smartphones.

_____

_____

5. ☐ In our search for constant connection, we have lost the art of conversation.

_____

_____

Write It!

Write three effective topic sentences using the topics from the Write It!
exercise on page 22. Make sure to include a controlling idea that makes a point
about your topic.

1. _____

_____

2. _____

_____

3. _____

_____

Supporting Ideas

When you have written a clear and effective topic sentence, you must think of ideas
that will prove, illustrate, or explain it. This is called support. To support your topic
sentence, you can use one or more of the following:

- **Facts and statistics** ▶ Relevant facts and statistics give authority to your ideas.
- **Examples** ▶ A relevant example is one of the best ways to support your topic.
- **Anecdotes** ▶ Everyone loves to read a good story. An anecdote can be an effective way to help your readers understand and remember your idea.
- **Quotations** ▶ Sometimes you will find that someone else, particularly an expert in the field, said what you want to say, but in a much better way. You can quote this person, but remember to acknowledge the source of your quotation.

Read the following paragraph and answer the questions that follow.

Texting while driving can have deadly consequences. I should know: it killed my best friend last summer. In the United States, texting and driving causes 1 600 000 accidents every year and 11 teen deaths every day. It is responsible for nearly 25% of all car accidents. In fact, texting while driving is even more dangerous than drinking and driving. Studies show that we are six times more likely to cause an accident if we text and drive than if we drink and drive. If you do not want to become one of these statistics, keep both of your hands on the wheel and do not text and drive.

1. Circle the topic of this paragraph and underline the controlling idea.

2. What is this sentence called? _____

3. What are the supporting sentences? Underline them twice.

4. Which of the four methods mentioned on the previous page does the author use to support her point of view?

_____

5. What is the conclusion? Put a star beside it.

6. What is the author's purpose in this paragraph?

_____

_____

7. Who is the intended audience?

_____

_____

Write It!

Write your own paragraph by chosing a topic sentence from the Write It! exercise on page 22. Use the following outline to guide your paragraph structure.

Topic: _____ Controlling idea: _____

Topic sentence: _____

Support 1: _____

_____

Support 2: _____

_____

Concluding sentence: _____

Revising and Editing

When you revise your paragraph, reread it to make sure all of your ideas are unified and cohesive. Then edit it by checking for mistakes and correcting them.

Revise and Edit It!

Revise the student paragraph below for content and structure. Use the paragraph checklist at the back of the book.

1. Rewrite the ineffective topic sentence.

_____

2. Find the supporting detail that does not belong in the paragraph. Cross it out.

3. Identify the concluding sentence. Is it effective?

_____

_____

4. Edit the paragraph for grammar and spelling, using the checklist at the back of the book. Underline and correct the ten errors in the paragraph (six errors in present tense verbs, two spelling errors, one punctuation error).

I love to play video games and I am not violent. First, the violence seen in video games are very unrealistic and never happens in real life. Most people who game are intelligent enough to know that they are play a video game and that it be not real life. In fact, everyone knowing that gaming is a stress-reliever and most people feel calmer after a good game. You can compare it to the endorphin release of going for a fast 5 km run? Running keeps me in really great shape and maybe that's why I am not violent. Finally, research show that most teenagers who becomes aggressive or violent after playing video games are usually violet to begin with. So please, stop blameing the video game industry for all the violence in our society.

Write It!

Apply the revision and editing strategies to the paragraph you wrote for the Write It! exercise on page 25.

PERSONALITY

Who Do You Think You Are?

Societal and family factors that affect your personality, life, and relationships

> Do you wonder what made you the person you are today?

> Who or what influenced you and shaped your values and personality?

> What is the nature versus nurture debate?

In this unit, you will learn more about how your generation, heritage, and family relationships contributed to create the person you are today.

Who is Generation Net?

What are the values that are important to you and your generation?

Discuss the survey questions with a partner and write your answers in the chart below. Then read the article on page 29 to find out how your answers compare with the rest of your generation's.

Survey Question	Your Answer	Partner's Answer
1. Are you optimistic about your future? Explain your answer.		
2. Do you believe in a god? Why or why not?		
3. Are you stressed? Why or why not?		
4. Who are the most important people in your life? Explain your answer.		
5. Do you think you have similar values and beliefs to your parents'? Explain your answer.		
6. Do you think you will get married and own a home? Why or why not?		
7. Do you work part-time? Why or why not?		
8. What are the most important problems facing youth today? List three.		

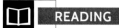
Maclean's magazine featured the results of several polls that describe your generation. How do your answers compare?

Read the poll results. Next to each result, write A if you agree or D if you disagree with the information.

Who Am I?

By Julia Belluz
Maclean's

You're not like your parents, but you confide in them. You've been stamped the iPod generation, but you believe in the power of print and that some technologies are evil. Recent polls provide a portrait of your generation.

5 **OPTIMISTIC** Seventy-nine per cent believe it's possible to create your destiny, and 52 per cent feel you will fulfill every one of your dreams. Almost all of you feel you will make it to graduation, and nearly two-thirds say you're engaged and enthusiastic about school.

10 **GODLESS** Is there a god? Not likely. You live in the moment, and probably do not participate in religion. In fact, your belief in science may trump your belief in a god.

RUSHED Time is the big stress. It drains your creativity.

FAST EATERS You spend more on fast food or takeout than 15 groceries.

LIBERAL Seventy-six per cent agree that 10 years from now "most people will be in support of interracial relationships," and 72 per cent agree that "non-traditional families will become accepted." Seventy-seven per cent agree that adoption 20 is "an acceptable way of creating a family."

FAMILY PEOPLE Family and friends are a top priority.

MOTHERS' DARLINGS Need advice? Most of you turn to mom and dad (33 per cent) over other confidants.

TECHNOPHOBIC? Surprise: you don't love technology 25 as much as others think. You feel Facebook and too much cellphone use have a negative impact on society.

UNIQUE You're not like mom and dad: 59 per cent feel your set of values and beliefs diverges from your parents'.

APOLITICAL Twenty-nine per cent don't have a political 30 preference or don't know, although you agree that democracy remains the best system of governance.

GIVING Volunteering is important, and you like to give back.

HOMEBODIES You want to own a home and have a good job.

RISK-AVERSE Unlike your parents, you're risk-averse, 35 especially when it comes to starting a business. Only 30 per cent anticipate starting a business, and just 33 per cent would rather lead than follow.

WEDDED Sixty-eight per cent of you expect to tie the knot in six to ten years and nearly three-quarters expect to have your 40 first child in that time period.

ANTI-DRUGS You think smoking, drugs, and alcohol are the most important problems facing youth today.

PART-TIME WORKERS You will likely get a job while at school in order to pay the bills.

45 **BROKE** A major concern is whether your money will run out, and four in ten of you say your money may not last beyond the end of the year.

FOCUSED After graduation, you'll probably go straight to the company you want to work for (48 per cent) instead of waiting 50 for an advertised position. Most of you have your sights set on a specific job or career (55 per cent) or hope to get a good job out of your studies (43 per cent).

472 words

Discussion

1. Are your values and beliefs reflected in these Canadian surveys? Which of the survey results match your own opinions most strongly? Explain your answer.

2. Which of the survey results differ from your own opinions most strongly? Explain your answer.

 How To

AGREE AND DISAGREE

I agree . . .	*I disagree that . . . because . . .*
I believe . . .	*I don't agree . . .*
You're right.	*I don't think that . . .*
That's true.	*That's not the case . . .*

Read "Who Do You Think You Are?" online to learn what Canadian comedian Shaun Majumder found when he traced his roots.

🗨 SPEAKING Tracing Your Roots

You may be a product of your generation, but how does your family heritage and past history influence who you are today? Learn more about your family's culture and history by tracing your roots.

Fill in the family tree below.

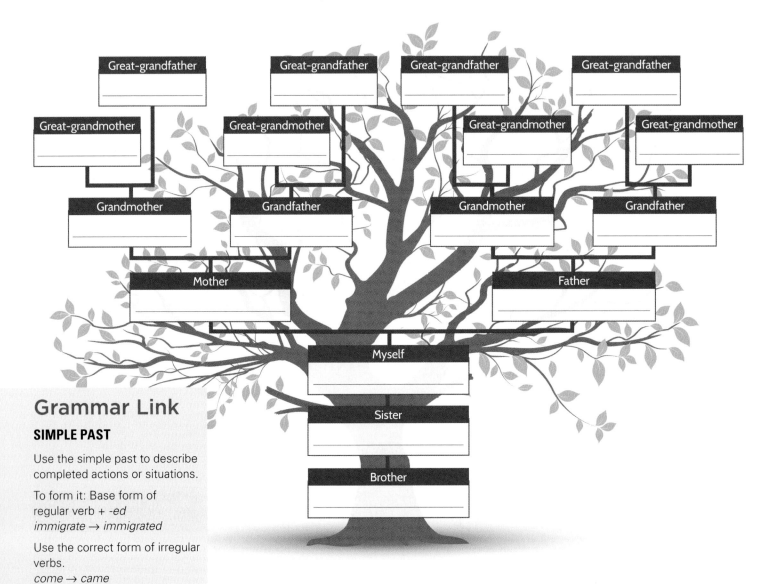

Grammar Link

SIMPLE PAST

Use the simple past to describe completed actions or situations.

To form it: Base form of regular verb + *-ed*
immigrate → immigrated

Use the correct form of irregular verbs.
come → came

*My grandparents **came** to Canada in 1948 after World War II.*

*They **immigrated** to Canada from the Netherlands. They **wanted** a better life for their children.*

▶ Refer to *REAL Grammar Book 2,* unit 4, and pages 134-135 for a list of irregular verbs.

Prepare a short presentation about your family origins. Tell your classmates where you are from and trace your family tree back as far as you can.

- Make sure to talk to your parents and grandparents to gather as much information as you can about your family history.

- Try to find and present at least two pieces of unique or especially interesting information about your family, for example your grandfather fought in a war, or you are related to Céline Dion.

- Explain how your family's history affects or defines your life today in terms of geography, education, career direction, or any other way you can think of.

◄◘► WATCHING 8th Fire: It's Time!

This CBC documentary explores the history of the First Nations and how it shaped and influenced modern Aboriginal culture.

Vocabulary

Match each word or expression with its definition before you watch the documentary.

1. to bring up (exp.)		a. financial aid provided by the government	
2. to grow up (exp.)		b. to take care of and educate	
3. a misconception (n.)		c. someone who quits school before graduating	
4. welfare (n.)		d. to become an adult	
5. to gain (v.)		e. official acceptance of status by another nation	
6. recognition (n.)		f. validation	
7. to improve (v.)		g. to obtain through an effort	
8. acknowledgement (n.)		h. the speed at which a population increases	
9. growth rate (n.)		i. a false idea	
10. a dropout (n.)		j. to make better	

Comprehension

Read the questions. Then watch the video and answer them.

1. Why does the comedian Howie Miller tell jokes?

_____

2. What do we learn about Howie Miller? Fill in the chart with the details you hear about him.

a. How many sons does he have? b. What "colour" is his wife?	c. Describe Miller's adoptive family.	d. What did Miller know about his culture as a child?	e. Who is his eldest son? Why is he famous?

3. Why does Tyson want to become a role model for Aboriginal youth?

_____

_____

4. List one of the complaints the men in the therapy group make about Aboriginal people.

_____

_____

5. How is the past history of the Cape Breton farmers of 1799 different from that of the Aboriginal people?

_____

_____

6. Fill in the blanks.

In 1982, the Supreme Court stated that if you want to do something on Indian land,

Aboriginal people have to be _____ ^{a} and _____ ^{b}.

7. How did the 2010 Olympics in British Columbia positively impact the Lil'wat First Nation? Name three ways.

• _____

• _____

• _____

8. What arguments does Paul Martin give about why we need to improve our relationship with Aboriginal people? Explain one of them.

_____

_____

Squamish Lil'wat Cultural Centre

9. Who is Vanessa? Fill in the chart with the details you hear about her life.

a. Describe Vanessa's youth.	b. How did Vanessa change her life?

10. Fill in the blanks in Vanessa's final quote.

"I really believe that where I _____ ^{a} from made me the woman

I am today. I am a strong _____ ^{b} woman and I won't let anything

stand in my way when I am _____ ^{c}. I'm here and I am going to do

_____ ^{d}."

(i+)

Watch *The Kid From La Puente* online to learn how Anthony Calvillo's challenging childhood led him to become a CFL football star.

Writing

Vanessa believes that where you come from makes you the person you are today. Reread her quote in question 10. Do you agree or disagree with her beliefs?

Write two paragraphs explaining the relationship between your family heritage and who you are today.

- Make sure that each paragraph has a clear topic sentence and support your statement with anecdotes and examples.
- Use the past tense when possible.

▶ Review paragraph form and function in Writing Files 1, page 21.

Pronunciation

The -ed Ending of Regular Verbs in the Simple Past

The -ed ending can be pronounced in three different ways.

/ t /	/ d /	/ id /
liked	learned	wanted

Listen to this tongue twister and repeat what you hear. Then, say it as quickly as you can.

Peter Piper picked a peck of pickled peppers.
A peck of pickled peppers Peter Piper picked.
If Peter Piper picked a peck of pickled peppers,
where's the peck of pickled peppers Peter Piper picked?

Listen to these verbs in the simple past. Repeat each verb aloud and write it in the correct column in the following chart.

/ t /	/ d /	/ id /

Discussion

Form small groups. Take turns describing an important event or person in your life that helped you become the person you are today.

- Use at least four regular verbs in the simple past (ending in -ed).
- Be careful to pronounce these verbs with their correct final sound.
- Designate another group member to write down the past tense verbs you use and to comment on your pronunciation of them when you finish.

How do our family relationships shape us? Read an excerpt from the coming-of-age book *The Perks of Being a Wallflower* by Stephen Chbosky to find out how the main character, Charlie, navigates family life.

The Perks of Being a Wallflower (Excerpt) By Stephen Chbosky

November 15, 1991

1 Dear Friend,
It's starting to get cold and frosty here. The pretty fall weather is pretty much gone. The good news is that we have holidays coming up, which I love especially now because my brother will be coming home soon. Maybe even for Thanksgiving! At least
5 I hope he does for my mom.

2 My brother hasn't called home in a few weeks now, and Mom just keeps talking about his grades and sleeping habits, and the foods he eats, and my dad keeps saying the same thing.

3 "He's not going to get **injured**."

4 10 Personally, I like to think my brother is having a college experience like they do in the movies. I don't mean the big fraternity party kind of movie. More like the movie where the guy meets a smart girl who wears a lot of sweaters and drinks cocoa. They talk about books and issues and kiss in the rain. I think something like that would be very good for him, especially if the girl were unconventionally beautiful. They are the best kind of girls, I think.
15 I personally find "super models" strange. I don't know why this is.

5 My brother, on the other hand, has posters of "super models" and cars and beer and things like that on the walls in his room. I suppose if you add a dirty floor, it's probably what his dorm room looks like. My brother always hated making his bed, but he kept his clothes closet very organized. Go figure.

6 20 The thing is, when my brother does call home, he doesn't say a lot. He talks about his classes a little bit, but mostly he talks about the football team. There is a lot of attention on the team because they are very good, and they have some really big players. My brother said that one of the guys will probably be a millionaire someday, but that he is "dumb as a post."

≫

injured (adj.) → hurt

My brother told this one story where the whole team was sitting around the **locker**
25 **room**, talking about all the stuff they had to do to get into college football. They finally got
around to talking about **SAT scores**, which I have never taken.

And this guy said, "I got a 710."

And my brother said, "Math or verbal?"

And the guy said, "Huh?"

30 And the whole team laughed

I always wanted to be on a sports team like that. I'm not exactly sure why, but I always
thought it would be fun to have "glory days." Then, I would have stories to tell my children
and golf buddies. I guess I could tell people about Punk Rocky and walking home from
school and things like that. Maybe these are my glory days, and I'm not even realizing it
35 because they don't involve a ball.

I used to play sports when I was little, and I was
actually very good, but the problem was that it used to
make me too aggressive, so the doctors told my mom
I would have to stop.

40 My dad had glory days once. I've seen pictures
of him when he was young. He was a very
handsome man. I don't know any other way to
put it. He looked like all old pictures look. Old pictures look very **rugged** and young, and the people
45 in the photographs always seem a lot happier than
you are.

My mother looks beautiful in old pictures. She actually looks more beautiful than
anyone except maybe **Sam**. Sometimes, I look at my parents now and wonder what
happened to make them the way they are. And then I wonder what will happen to my
50 sister when her boyfriend graduates from law school. And what my brother's face will look
like on a football card, or what it will look like if it is never on a football card. My dad played
college baseball for two years, but he had to stop when Mom got **pregnant** with my brother.
That's when he started working at the office. I honestly don't know what my dad does.

He tells a story sometimes. It is a great story. It has to do with the state championship
55 for baseball when he was in high school. It was the bottom of the ninth inning, and there
was a runner on first. There were two outs, and my dad's team was behind by one run. My
dad was younger than most of the varsity team because he was only a **sophomore** and I
think the team thought he was going to **blow** the game. He had all this pressure on him. He
was really nervous. And really scared. But after a few pitches, he said he started feeling "in
60 the zone." When the pitcher wound up and threw the next ball, he knew exactly where that
ball was going to be. He hit it harder than any other ball he ever hit in his whole life. And he
made a **home run**, and his team won the state championship. The greatest thing about this
story is that every time my dad tells it, it never changes. He's not one to exaggerate.

I think about all this sometimes when I'm watching a football game with Patrick and
65 Sam. I look at the field, and I think that these are the glory days for that boy, and this
moment will just be another story someday because all the people who make touchdowns
and home runs will become somebody's dad. And when his children look at his yearbook
photograph, they will think that their dad was rugged and handsome and looked a lot
happier than they are.

70 I just hope I remember to tell my kids that they are as happy as I look in my old
photographs. And I hope that they believe me.
Love always,
Charlie

975 words

---

7 **locker room** (n.) → room next to
the gymnasium for changing your
clothes

8
9 **SAT scores** (n.) → results of
10 standardized tests used for
11 admission to American
12 universities

13

14

"So, I guess we are who we are for a lot of reasons. And
maybe we'll never know most of them. But even if we don't
have the power to choose where we come from, we can
still choose wherever we go from there. We can still do
things. And we can try to feel okay about them."

From *The Perks of Being a Wallflower*

15

rugged (adj.) → strong, robust

Sam (n.) → short for Samantha

pregnant (adj.) → having a baby
developing in the body

16

sophomore (n.) → second-year
student

blow (v.) → ruin

home run (n.) → hit in baseball that
allows the batter to score

17

18

Vocabulary

Find the word or expression in the text that matches the definition. The paragraph number is in parentheses.

Definition	Word or Expression
1. beautiful (1)	
2. almost (1)	
3. marks you get at school (2)	
4. bizarre (3)	
5. college residence (5)	
6. expresses confusion over something contradictory (5)	
7. not intelligent (6)	
8. describes a past habitual action (13)	

📖 How To

MAKE INFERENCES

Inferences are ideas or opinions that are not stated but that can and should be understood (inferred) from the information given. Making inferences is also known as *reading between the lines.*

When you infer, you go beyond the surface information to see other meanings that the writer suggests or implies but does not state explicitly.

For example, Charlie, the narrator, never overtly describes himself in this passage. However, readers can use their inferencing skills to learn about him.

Inferencing and Comprehension

1. Find the context in the story that supports the inferences about Charlie.

Inference	Context
a. Charlie is a high-school student.	
b. Charlie is romantic.	
c. Charlie is interested in Sam.	
d. Charlie is proud of his brother.	
e. Charlie is nostalgic.	

2. Based on what Charlie says and implies about his family members, give a brief description of each person.

a. Brother	b. Sister	c. Mother	d. Father

3. Describe the type of girlfriend Charlie wants his brother to have. Describe the type of girlfriend Charlie's brother probably has.

4. Make inferences about the "glory days."

   a. What are *glory days*?

   b. Why are *glory days* important?

   c. Why does Charlie know his father's glory day moment but not what he does at the office every day? Explain your answer.

Focus on Language: Past Tenses

1. Read this passage from paragraph 7 and analyze the verb tenses. Fill in the chart below with the verbs in bold and explain why the tense is used.

   *My brother **told** this one story where the whole team **was sitting** around the*

   *locker room, talking about all the stuff they **had** to do to get into college football.*

   *They finally **got** around to talking about SAT scores, which I have never taken.*

Verb Tense	Verbs from Passage	Why the Tense Is Used
a. simple past		
b. past progressive		

Writing

Write a journal entry describing one of the following:

- a recent conflict you had with your brother or sister, or someone you are very close to, how you resolved it, and what you learned from it
- a recent great moment (or glory day) that you had and what you learned about life from this event

Make sure to use past tenses where appropriate. Edit your work for correct spelling, grammar, and punctuation.

How To

WRITE A JOURNAL ENTRY

Journal writing allows you to be actively engaged with your life, to reflect on it, and to write about the result of that reflection. Write exactly what you are thinking without fear of being judged.

- Write in the first person as much as possible.
- Use vivid language.
- Reflect upon events and explain your thoughts and beliefs.

Idioms

Family

Is it true that blood is thicker than water? Learn some common idiomatic expressions we often use to talk about our family ties.

Complete the idiomatic expression with its missing final word from the word box. With a partner, try to guess what each expression means.

block	relationship
blood	roost
buttons	tango
family	water

Idiom	Meaning
1. blood is thicker than _____water_____	Family bonds are stronger than bonds between unrelated people.
2. it runs in the _____	
3. it takes two to _____	
4. my own flesh and _____	
5. to push my _____	
6. close-knit _____	
7. a chip off the old _____	
8. to rule the _____	

💬 SPEAKING Birth Order

Partners and friends come and go, but siblings are with us for a long time. Did you know that birth order and siblings could influence your personality, success, and life choices?

Discuss the following with a partner or in small groups. Make sure to use two idioms to describe your sibling relationships.

1. If you have a sibling or siblings, describe:
   • your sibling's personality and physical traits
   • your relationship with your sibling
   • how your birth order (e.g. first-born, middle child, youngest) influences your personality and life choices

2. If you are an only child, describe:
   • the advantages of being an only child
   • the disadvantages of being an only child
   • how being an only child influences your personality or life choices

3. If you are a twin, describe:
   • your sibling's personality and physical traits
   • your relationship with your twin
   • how being a twin influences your personality and life choices

🎧 LISTENING The Sibling Effect

How do relationships with siblings shape the person you become? This "On Point" interview with Jeffrey Kluger, author of *The Sibling Effect: What the Bonds Among Brothers and Sisters Reveal About Us*, explores these important relationships.

Decide if you think these statements are truths or myths before you listen to the interview. Discuss your beliefs with a partner.

	Truth	Myth
1. Children spend more time with their siblings than with anybody else.		
2. When we are young, we fight with our siblings every 10 minutes.		
3. Fighting with siblings gives us real-life skills.		
4. Our sibling relationships do more to define us than our relationship with our parents.		
5. First-born children are usually more successful.		
6. The youngest sibling is generally the smartest.		
7. Younger siblings are more charismatic.		
8. Middle children have higher self-esteem.		

Practise listening to English as often as you can, for short amounts of time. Try listening to the radio in the car or watching your favourite comedy or reality show in English.

Accept the fact that you will not understand every word or phrase you hear. Stay calm and remind yourself that the ultimate goal is to understand the main ideas. If you don't understand completely, try to guess the meaning from the context.

Don't translate into your mother tongue. This will slow you down and prevent you from understanding what the speaker is saying.

Vocabulary

Listen to the introduction to the interview and fill in the blanks with the words you hear. Then, write a synonym or short definition in parentheses for each missing word.

"You might remember the early days of _____ [1] (_____)

with your siblings. Running, jumping, screaming, growing up. They were antagonists,

_____ [2] (_____), confidants, best friends. Maybe they

propped you up when others _____ [3] (_____).

Maybe they pulled you down, when you wanted to _____ [4]

(_____). A new book looks at how _____ [5]

(_____) shape the adults we become."

Comprehension

Listen to the rest of the interview and answer these questions.

1. How often do we fight with our siblings?

   _____

   _____

2. What do we learn from fighting with our siblings?

   _____

3. Why does it matter that we fight with our siblings and not our friends or classmates?

   _____

   _____

4. Listen to what the expert says about the characteristics of birth order and take detailed notes about what you hear.

a. Eldest	b. Youngest	c. Middle

5. Return to the Truth or Myth activity on page 39. Correct your answers based on what the expert explained in this interview.

📖 **READING** **FOR CHALLENGE**

What has a greater influence on who we are: genes or the environment? Is it nature or nurture? This *National Geographic* article explains how identical twins are helping scientists answer the questions.

Vocabulary

Match each word or expression with its definition before you read the text. The line number is in parentheses.

1.	to split (v., 3)	a.	a route through life
2.	to shape (v., 9)	b.	far from one another
3.	a path (n., 23)	c.	to separate
4.	to set out (v., 30)	d.	to create, define, form
5.	outgoing (adj., 32)	e.	timid
6.	shy (adj., 32)	f.	to begin
7.	related (adj., 56)	g.	sociable and responsive to others
8.	apart (adv., 62)	h.	connected by family ties

A Thing or Two About Twins

By Peter Miller
National Geographic

To scientists, and to biomedical researchers all over the world, twins offer an opportunity to **untangle** the influence of genes and the environment—of nature and nurture. Because identical twins come from a single fertilized egg that splits in two, they share the same genetic code. Any differences between them must be due to environmental factors.

5 Lately, however, twin studies have helped lead scientists to a radical, almost **heretical**, new conclusion: that nature and nurture are not the only elemental forces at work. According to a recent field called *epigenetics*, there is a third factor also in play, one that in some cases serves as a bridge between the environment and our genes, and in others operates on its own to shape who we are.

10 The story began with the much publicized case of two brothers, both named Jim. Born in Piqua, Ohio, in 1939, Jim Springer and Jim Lewis were put up for adoption as babies and raised by different couples, who happened to give them the same first name. When Jim Springer reconnected with his brother at age 39 in 1979, they uncovered a **string** of other similarities and coincidences. Both men were 1.83 m tall and weighed 81.6 kg. Growing up,

15 they'd both had dogs named Toy and taken family vacations in St. Pete Beach in Florida. As young men, they'd both married women named Linda, and then divorced them. Their second wives were both named Betty. They named their sons James Alan and James Allan. They'd both served as part-time sheriffs, enjoyed home carpentry projects, suffered severe headaches, smoked Salem cigarettes, and drank Miller Lite beer.

untangle (v.) → resolve or clarify

heretical (adj.) → unorthodox

string (n.) → series

>>

Twins Lily and Gillian were separated at birth. They are being raised by different adoptive families in different cities but see each other every six to eight weeks

20   As soon as he heard about the two Jims, Thomas Bouchard, Jr., a psychologist at the University of Minnesota, invited them to his lab in Minneapolis. There he and his team gave the brothers a series of tests that confirmed their similarities. Although each had charted his own course in life, the Jim twins seemed to have followed the same paths.

     Researchers discovered other twins who'd been separated as infants and reunited 25 as adults. Over two decades, 137 sets of twins eventually visited Bouchard's lab in what became known as the Minnesota Study of Twins Reared Apart. The twins were tested for mental skills, such as vocabulary, visual memory, arithmetic, and spatial rotation. They were given lung-function tests and heart exams and had their brain waves measured. They took personality tests and **IQ** tests and were quizzed about their sexual histories.

30   Armed with this mountain of data, Bouchard, Segal, and their colleagues set out to **unravel** some of the biggest mysteries of human nature: Why are some people happy and others sad? Why are some outgoing and others shy? Where does general intelligence come from? The key to their approach was a statistical concept called heritability. In broad terms, the heritability of a trait measures the extent to which differences among members of a 35 population can be explained by differences in their genetics.

     When they looked at the data on twins' intelligence, Bouchard's team reached a controversial conclusion: For people raised in the same culture with the same opportunities, differences in **IQ** reflected largely differences in inheritance rather than in training or education.

40   The researchers also questioned how much parenting affects intelligence levels. When they compared identical twins raised in different families, like the Jim twins, with those raised in the same family, they found each pair's IQ scores to be similar. It was as if it didn't matter in which family the twins had been raised.

     For two couples in Canada, the power of DNA to affect behaviour is more than an 45 academic question. Since 2000, they've been raising identical twin sisters 443 km apart in a kind of accidental science experiment.

     Lynette and Mike Shaw met Allyson and Kirk MacLeod while using the same adoption agency. The Shaws live in Amherstburg, a rural community near Windsor, Ontario, and the MacLeods live in Sutton, a suburban town near Toronto. In February 2000, they travelled 50 together to Chenzhou, China.

     "When the girls came out of the elevator, we looked at our daughter and the other child, and I went, "Wow, she looks just the same," Mike says "Their cries were the same. Their laughs were the same. You honestly couldn't tell one baby girl from the other," Lynette adds.

     Before coming to China, the couples had seen photographs of the infants, who were 55 six months old at the time, and they'd wondered if they were sisters. When they asked representatives of the orphanage, they were told the girls weren't related, even though they were listed as having the same birth date. The couples were told both children would not be given to a single family for adoption. If the Shaws and MacLeods did not adopt them, the babies would be returned to the orphanage and placed with other families. Under such 60 circumstances, the couples feared, the girls might be separated forever. So they took the babies home to Canada with them, determined to do what was best, even if that meant raising identical twin sisters apart.

     The MacLeods make the four-hour drive to Amherstburg—or the Shaws travel to Sutton—every six to eight weeks. Because they've kept in close touch, the parents have 65 shared every milestone they've tracked in the twins' development. At 14 months old, for example, both girls took their first steps on the same day—one in Amherstburg, the other in Sutton. They both had small holes in their teeth and amblyopia, or lazy eye, in one eye. Even as toddlers, they both showed the same aggressive streak.

     As they grew older, Lily seemed to be the artistic one, Gillian the athlete, spurred on 70 perhaps by the Shaw's other children, Heather and Eric, who were both into sports. "But then Lily went out for track and won her hundred metres," Kirk says. "And I came back to that nature versus nurture thing."

     A geneticist by training, Danielle Reed has worked with many twins over the years and thought deeply about what twin studies have taught us. "It's very clear when you look at twins

>>

75 that much of what they share is hardwired," she says. "Many things about them are absolutely the same and **unalterable**. But it's also clear, when you get to know them, that other things about them are different. Epigenetics is the origin of a lot of those differences in my view."

Having said that, Reed adds, the latest work in epigenetics promises to take our understanding even further. "What I like to say is that Mother Nature writes some things
80 in pencil and some things in pen," she says. "Things written in pen you can't change. That's DNA. But things written in pencil you can. That's epigenetics. Now that we're actually able to look at the DNA and see where the pencil writings are, it's sort of a whole new world."

unalterable (adj.) → unchangeable

1148 words

Comprehension

1. Why are scientists so interested in studying twins? What can twin studies tell us about human nature?

   _____

   _____

   _____

2. What is the difference between *nature* and *nurture*?

   _____

   _____

3. Who are the "Jim twins" and why are they so fascinating?

   _____

   _____

   _____

   _____

4. By studying twins raised apart, what are some important questions scientists want to answer?

   _____

   _____

5. By analysing twin data, what did the researchers conclude about intelligence?

   _____

   _____

6. What does the Chinese adoption story contribute to the nature versus nurture debate?

   _____

   _____

7. What is epigenetics and what can it tell us about ourselves?

   _____

   _____

Doubles team members Mike (at left) and Bob Bryan anticipate each other's moves so well they have won 70 tennis championships.

Write a text or give an oral presentation on one of the following topics. Try to incorporate the elements seen in the unit from the Make the Connection box and use as many of the Top Words as you can, where appropriate.

Make the Connection

- ☐ Simple past and past progressive
- ☐ Vocabulary and idioms from the unit
- ☐ Pronouncing the -*ed* ending of regular verbs in the simple past
- ☐ Agreeing and disagreeing
- ☐ Inferencing
- ☐ Journal writing
- ☐ Writing coherent paragraphs and topic sentences

▶ Refer to Writing Files 1, page 21, for information on paragraphs.

▶ Refer to appendix 1, page 155, for information on oral presentations.

Vocabulary from the unit and other theme-related vocabulary can be practised online.

1 **GENERATION NET:** How is your generation different from your parents' generation? Interview your parents or your grandparents about their youth. Who do you think has, or had, the better youth?

2 **ABORIGINAL CULTURE:** Research an aspect of aboriginal culture or history. How do you think this aspect influenced the aboriginal culture of today? What kinds of laws are appropriate to protect this culture?

3 **BIRTH ORDER:** Are you the first-born, middle or youngest, or an only child? How does birth order shape your personality and your career goals?

4 **FAMILY HISTORY:** Where did you come from? How does your family's history define the person you are today?

5 **NATURE VS. NURTURE:** Is it heredity or the environment? Which factor do you think plays a greater role in creating the person you are today?

6 **OTHER:** _____ Write about another topic of your choice linked to what you learned in this unit. Make sure to have your topic approved by your teacher.

Top Words

Put a check mark next to the words you know and refer to the page numbers in the unit to learn the ones you don't know. Add to the list other words you want to remember from the unit.

ADJECTIVES	NOUNS	VERBS	EXPRESSIONS
☐ **outgoing** (41)	☐ **a dropout** (31)	☐ **to gain** (31)	☐ **to bring up** (31)
☐ **pretty** (36)	☐ **fighting** (40)	☐ **to improve** (31)	☐ **to grow up** (31)
☐ **related** (41)	☐ **grades** (36)	☐ **to shape** (41)	☐ **to put down** (40)
☐ **shy** (41)	☐ **playmates** (40)	☐ **to shine** (40)	☐ **used to** (36)
☐ **strange** (36)	☐ **recognition** (31)	☐ **to split** (41)	
	☐ **siblings** (39)		

OTHER:

_____   _____

_____   _____

_____   _____

_____   _____

How Far Will You Go and Why?

How travel and adventure can change us and transform communities

> Where will you go on your next adventure?

> Will you climb to the top of Machu Picchu, sunbathe on a beach in Mexico, or paraglide from the highest mountains of Nepal?

> Does your dream vacation involve helping others, learning more about yourself, or just getting away from it all?

In this unit, you will learn more about the transforming powers of travel.

LET'S HIT THE ROAD!

 **WARM-UP** # What's Your Travel Style?

How do you like to travel? There are so many different travel styles. Some people dream of relaxing in a hammock under a palm tree, while others prefer to climb to the top of Mount Everest.

Take the following quiz to learn more about your personal travel style. Fill in the missing verbs (*is, are, do,* and *will*) before you answer the questions.

1. How adventurous _____ you consider yourself? Rate yourself on a scale of 1 to 5 by circling the number that best describes you.

Very adventurous		Somewhat adventurous		Not adventurous
5	4	3	2	1

2. Where _____ you probably go on your next trip? (List three countries or cities.)

   _____ _____ _____

3. What _____ your favourite activities when you travel? Check two.
   ☐ Visiting museums and historical sites ☐ Speaking a different language
   ☐ Hiking, trekking, and cycling ☐ Photographing or watching wildlife
   ☐ Trying restaurants and local foods ☐ Beach activities, water sports
   ☐ Meeting local people ☐ Other: _____

4. When you travel, what _____ your preferred modes of transportation? Check two.
   ☐ Walking ☐ Bus ☐ Plane
   ☐ **Hitchhiking** ☐ Car ☐ Cruise ship
   ☐ Bicycle ☐ Train ☐ 4×4 vehicle

5. What _____ your priorities when you travel? Check two.
   ☐ Laundry facilities to keep my clothes clean
   ☐ A book, iPod, or MP3 player to enjoy during **downtime**
   ☐ A structured tour with many planned activities
   ☐ A stay in a small village, learning about new cultures
   ☐ Reliable electricity for keeping all my essential items powered up
   ☐ Access to email and maintaining contact
   ☐ Free time to explore and enjoy things on my own
   ☐ Physical challenges that push me to the limit
   ☐ A peaceful environment where I can just relax
   ☐ Good food and drink

6. What _____ your preference for sleeping accommodations?
   ☐ Anywhere ☐ Someone's sofa ☐ A small hotel with character
   ☐ A tent in the wild ☐ A youth hostel ☐ Expensive lodges and resorts

7. How long _____ your ideal trip?
   ☐ One week ☐ Two to three weeks ☐ More than one month
   ☐ One to two weeks ☐ One month

hitchhiking (n.) → soliciting free rides along a road

downtime (n.) → time for relaxing

Watch "Real-World Adventures" to learn about unique tours designed by the Canadian company G.A.P. Adventures.

8. Who _____ you prefer to travel with?
- ☐ My family
- ☐ My friends
- ☐ On my own
- ☐ Big groups of strangers, for more chances to make friends
- ☐ Small groups of close friends, for more intimate experiences
- ☐ Groups of people around my age

9. What _____ your level of physical activity when you travel?
- ☐ I try to avoid physical activity as much as possible.
- ☐ I expect to do a variety of physical activities, but nothing too strenuous.
- ☐ I enjoy just about anything: hiking, biking, horseback riding, kayaking, and more.
- ☐ I want a real physical challenge. No pain, no gain!

10. What type of travel budget _____ you have?
- ☐ All-inclusive: I want to pay in advance and have everything included in the price.
- ☐ I enjoy choosing and paying for my own meals and activities.
- ☐ I want my hotel rooms and transportation included in the price and I budget for everything else.
- ☐ I don't have much money so I prefer to find free accommodation by using a travel network like couchsurfing.

Interview a classmate to learn about his or her travel style. Find out about his or her travel plans. Use the questions above as a guide for your discussion, or make up your own questions. Use the future in your questions and answers.

Describe your partner's travel style and travel plans to a small group of classmates. Study the travel vocabulary box below before you begin. Don't forget to pronounce the -s at the end of third-person singular verbs.

> Brian is an adventure traveller. He hopes to travel to Costa Rica. He **is going to learn** how to surf. He **will** probably **spend** about one month there. For this trip, he does not have a lot of money, so he **will** most likely **bike** and **camp**.

Travel Vocabulary

To talk about your travel adventures, you need to know the difference between these words:

Travel is used to talk about going from one place to another.
Verb ▶ *Melissa often travels for her job.*
Noun ▶ *Travel is a life-changing experience.*
Adjective ▶ *This travel guide is very helpful.*
▶ *I ~~made a travel~~ to Europe.* ▶ *I travelled to Europe.*

A trip (n.) is used to talk about a relatively short journey for a purpose, either business or pleasure.
▶ *My parents took me on a trip to Florida.*
▶ *My mom takes many business trips every year.*

A journey (n.) means the distance covered in travelling from one place to another.
▶ *The journey was long and tiring. It took 10 hours to get to New York.*

A voyage (n.) refers to a long journey by sea or in space.
▶ *Before the 20th century, long sea voyages were common.*

Grammar Link
THE FUTURE

Use *will* or *be going to* to talk about future actions. Both forms are generally acceptable.
*Where **will** you **go** on your next vacation?*
*Where **are** you **going to go** on your next vacation?*

There are some distinctions in meaning. Use *be going to* to talk about planned actions or intentions.
*I'm going to visit New York City on a school trip. We **are going to see** the Statue of Liberty.*

Use *will* for spontaneous decisions or promises.
I'll come with you! We'll be on time.

Both are used for predictions.
*We **will have** a great time.*
*We **are going to have** a great time.*

▶ Refer to *REAL Grammar Book 2*, unit 5.

Practise this travel vocabulary online.

◉ WATCHING   Skyward Journey

Some travellers like to push themselves to the limit when they travel. This award-winning short film was shot in the Khumbu region of Nepal. It follows adventure traveller Rex Pemberton as he takes his paragliding to new heights.

Look at the following photos of adventure travel before you watch the video. With a partner, describe and name the activity represented in each photo. Try to guess where each photo was taken.

Discussion

1. Will you do any of these adventures someday? Why or why not?

2. Why are some people attracted to extreme adventures?

3. In which cases can the risk of the activity outweigh the reward?

4. Should there be places in the world where adventure travel is not allowed? Why or why not?

Vocabulary

Watch the first part of the video and complete the text with the words you hear. Then match each word with a synonym or definition from the box on the left. Write the corresponding letter in the parentheses.

My parents always encouraged us to open our hearts and our _____ ¹ (___) to the world, to be inspired, to live creatively, and to push the scope of our _____ ² (___) through adventure, through exploring our passions. My childhood really was where my love for adventure _____ ³ (___). As a kid, I always walked the _____ ⁴ (___) looking up at the high mountains, and looking up at the _____ ⁵ (___), wondering what it would be like to _____ ⁶ (___) that, wondering what it would be like to _____ ⁷ (___). Now I know what it's like. I lived my _____ ⁸ (___).

Read "Who Should Pay for Rescuing Wayward Adventurers" online for another perspective on the issue of adventure travel.

a. cherished desire
b. began
c. limitations
d. planet
e. brains
f. where we find clouds
g. soar
h. ascend

Comprehension

Watch the rest of the video and answer these questions.

1. How many summits did Rex climb?

_____

2. Why did Rex start to paraglide?

_____

_____

3. How does Rex describe the first time he tried paragliding?

_____

4. Why did Rex travel to the mountains?

_____

_____

5. How does Rex describe his relationship with his camera?

_____

_____

6. When is the best time to fly in Nepal, according to Rex? Why?

_____

7. How does Rex describe Nepal?

_____

8. What is his dream come true?

_____

9. Rex tells us about one of his "wild times" in Nepal. What is he describing?

_____

_____

10. Rex describes his life philosophy. What does he say he lives for?

_____

_____

11. Is Rex happy with the way he lives his life? Explain your answer.

_____

_____

Pronunciation

The /th/ Sound

To pronounce the /th/ sound in English, place the tip of your tongue at the bottom of your top teeth and blow air out of your mouth. If you don't pronounce the /th/ sound correctly, it can sometimes lead to confusion.

He taught about travelling.

But what you meant to say was:

He thought about travelling.

Listen to this tongue twister and repeat what you hear. Then say it as quickly as you can.

I thought a thought.
But the thought I thought wasn't the thought
I thought I thought.

Listen carefully to these sentences and circle the words you hear. Then repeat the sentence after the speaker.

1. He has a big (mouse/mouth).

2. I feel very (sick/thick).

3. The general said to send in many (tanks/thanks).

4. He (taught/thought) for a little while.

5. This (bat/bath) is too big.

6. John came in (tent/tenth).

7. You look very (thin/fin).

8. By which (path/pass) did you (path/pass)?

9. There are (three/tree) boys standing over by that (tree/three).

10. The passengers didn't (sink/think).

Practise your pronunciation of the /th/ sound. Read these phrases and sentences from the *Skyward Journey* video aloud to a partner or to your teacher.

1. " . . . to push the scope of our boundaries, **th**rough adventure, **th**rough exploring our passions . . ."

2. ". . . I always walked **the earth** looking up at **the** high mountains."

3. "I really live for **the** love of **th**is planet, for **the** people wi**th**in it."

4. " I always **th**ought **th**ere was a better way to get off **these** mountains . . ."

5. "And I love **the th**ought of **that**."

At 21 years old, Tori Holmes became the youngest woman to row across an ocean. She crossed the Atlantic Ocean in an eight-metre boat in eighty-five days. Read this description of her journey.

Getting Meaning from Context

Write a short definition, synonym, or translation of each word in bold on the lines provided. Use context clues to guess the meaning of each word.

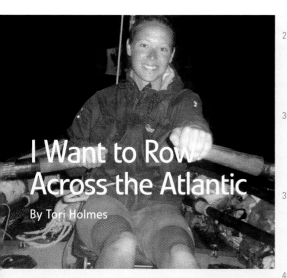

I Want to Row Across the Atlantic

By Tori Holmes

I'm such an **average Joe**[1]. Anyone who grew up with me in my small hometown in Alberta would have described me that way—I'm 158 cm with strawberry blond hair,
5 and come from a pretty normal family. In high school I was kind of an **overachiever**[2], playing every sport and hanging out with every group. The truth was that I was a master of disguise. No one knew—I didn't know—that I was
10 severely dyslexic until almost the end of my time in high school. For years I had just been learning how to learn, hiding the fact that I thought I was stupid. I was very good at achieving, but I had incredibly low self-esteem.
15 I think that was the real motivator behind my trip with Paul. I went out there with the thought, "If I can do this, I can do anything. I can teach myself not to be stupid." You know that Robert Frost poem about the two
20 roads diverging in a yellow wood? I'd always wanted to take the other road. Getting into a tiny rowboat and crossing the Atlantic, with just one other person to rely on for almost three months, was my other road.

25 Just getting to the boat was an ordeal itself. You have to sit down and think, "Am I selfish enough to do this?" You have to look your parents in the eye and tell them that you'll be risking your life, that there is
30 no plan B out there. You either finish or you almost definitely die.

My parents didn't really understand, but they were willing to support me. But when you wake up after just an hour and
35 a half of sleep to pull the midnight to 2:00 a.m. shift, and it's so dark you can't see your hand in front of your face, and you step out of the cabin and just freeze in terror because the ocean is so big and dark and you're so
40 **alone**[3], your parents aren't there to help you. No one is. Your partner needs to rest, so he's inside the cabin. Even if the boat **capsizes**[4], he can't come out to see if you're okay, or you'll just both end up lost at sea.

45 One night I watched as a wave rose up and curled over our two-metre-tall cabin and hit me right in the face. It was like being attacked by a wild animal. I went over the side, and all Paul saw was my feet going into the **white**
50 **wash**[5]. He couldn't turn the boat around or he'd risk his own life, too, so he had to watch and wait. I was **harnessed**[6] to the boat, as always, and somehow I pulled myself back in.

But I'd been thrown so hard (I'd hit
55 the water and the bottom of the boat) that, though I didn't know it at the time, I'd broken several ribs and bruised my gallbladder. I was puking up blood and the pain was indescribable. We had a satellite phone,
60 which didn't always work, but we managed to reach a friend who was a nursing student at the time. She **talked me through**[7] the first-aid kit we had. Somehow she figured out that my **unrelenting**[8] nausea would be
65 helped if I ate toothpaste. I ate a whole tube.

How To

GET MEANING FROM CONTEXT

An effective reading strategy is to guess the meaning of unknown words based on your understanding of the context. When you come across an unknown word:

1. Analyse the word. Do you recognize part of it? If yes, you may be able to guess the rest.
   light bulb, **usual**ly

2. Understand the part of speech. Knowing the function of the word can help you to guess its meaning.
   The nurse **records** (verb) the patient's results and then files them with the other hospital **records** (noun).

3. Study the surrounding words and sentences. You will find context clues that may help you guess the meaning of the word.
   When you **wake up** after just an hour and a half of sleep **to pull** the midnight to 2:00 a.m. shift . . .
   Could you guess that wake up means to stop sleeping and to pull means to do or perform?

1. _____

2. _____

3. _____

4. _____

5. _____

6. _____

7. _____

8. _____

My dad and I have always had a special **bond**[9]. The row was especially hard for him because he was working in a mine in the Northwest Territories and couldn't even follow
70 our progress online. He was underground, **cut off**[10] from everything. But one night he woke up with an overwhelming vision of me drowning. He went to the main office and sent me this message: "Push through the pain. Face
75 the fear to Valhalla and back. You're a Viking!"

And just a few hours later I'd been thrown from the boat and I thought I was going to die from the **injuries**[11] I couldn't even really diagnose. I was lying in the cabin, vomiting
80 and in incredible pain. But I thought, "If I don't get up and row, I'll be out here even longer." So I ate that toothpaste. I got up (and vomited again) and got back to rowing.

For three or four weeks, twelve hours
85 a day, I rowed through the pain. It was like watching someone else. I just disassociated from it. And I kept repeating those words my dad had sent: "Push through the pain. Face the fear to Valhalla and back. You're a Viking!"
90 There wasn't a plan B. I hadn't gone out there to die.

I didn't think I'd see my dad at the end of the race; he couldn't get the time off work.
95 But the morning we came in, he was there. He'd gotten up at 5:00 a.m., just to watch us come over the horizon. Seeing him on the **shore**[12] was the most emotional moment of my life.

100 It wasn't anything supernatural, the way he'd saved me. It was just the connection between a parent and his child. I was all the way on the other side of the world, but my dad could feel my danger, and he had
105 the instinct to protect and help. I learned so much about myself on that trip and every day I carry the quiet confidence that comes from knowing what my limits really are. But through that harrowing time, it was my dad
110 whose strength got me through. I borrowed his **strength**[13] to survive.

914 words

Two roads diverged in a yellow wood,
And sorry I could not travel both
And be one traveller, long I stood
And looked down one as far as I could
. . .
Two roads diverged in a wood, and I—
I took the one less travelled by,
And that has made all the difference.

Excerpt from *The Road Not Taken*
by Robert Frost

1. What does the writer mean by calling one road "the one less travelled by"?

2. Why do you think the writer said his choice "has made all the difference"?

Comprehension

1. Why does Tori describe herself as an "average Joe"?

_____

2. What secret was she hiding? How did this make her feel? How did this contribute to her decision to cross the Atlantic?

_____

_____

_____

_____

3. Name one of Tori's fears.

_____

4. Describe Tori's accident and her subsequent injuries.

_____

_____

5. What did she eat to help relieve her nausea? _____

6. Describe Tori's relationship with her father? How did he help to "save" her?

_____

_____

7. What did Tori learn from her adventure?

_____

_____

8. Do you think she took too much of a risk by taking this trip? Why or why not?

_____

Focus on Descriptive Writing

Read lines 45–53 and underline all the descriptive words and expressions that help you experience Tori's adventure. Fill in the following chart with what you see, taste, feel, smell, and hear.

1. See	2. Taste	3. Feel	4. Smell	5. Hear

Writing

Write a story about an adventure that had a lasting effect on you. Use descriptive language that appeals to the five senses so that readers can experience the adventure, too.

How To

WRITE A THESIS STATEMENT FOR A STORY

When you write a story, begin by asking yourself what you learned from the events described in your narrative, how it was important, or how it affected you. The answer to one of these questions will become your thesis statement.

When I skied out of bounds at Whistler and was caught in an avalanche, I learned that I am not invincible.

My volunteer trip to Guatemala taught me to be happy with less.

When I was a camp monitor, not only did I teach something to children, I learned from them.

Refer to Writing Files 2, page 65, for more information on thesis statements.

Travel

Hit the road, Jack! English is full of idiomatic expressions that we use when we talk about travel.

Look at the literal meanings of the idioms below.

1. to know something like the back of your hand → to know something very well
2. 9 a.m. sharp → at 9 a.m. exactly
3. to travel light → to go on a journey without taking a lot of things with you
4. to be in good hands → to be taken care of by a responsible person
5. to be smooth sailing → to encounter no problems
6. to cross that bridge when you come to it → to deal with that problem when it occurs
7. to be down-to-earth → to be a sensible, practical person
8. to be an early bird → to wake up and get out of bed early in the morning
9. to take it easy → to relax
10. to hit the hay → to go to bed

Read the dialogue and complete it with the correct idiomatic expressions. Then role-play the dialogue with a partner and practise saying the idiomatic expressions correctly.

Jamie and Sabrina are making the final arrangements for their eco-adventure to the Galapagos Islands.

Jamie: Sabrina, I know that you have trouble waking up in the morning because you're

not an _____ [1], but our plane leaves at 7:00 a.m.

_____ [2]. This means that we have to leave our

house at 4:00 a.m.

Sabrina: What happens if we get lost at the airport?

Jamie: Don't worry, Sabrina. I know the airport _____ [3].
I used to work there. We won't get lost!

Sabrina: I'm excited about our adventure, but I'm worried that I'll be really homesick.

Jamie: Yeah, I know what you mean, but we will _____ [4].
We can't worry about that now.

Sabrina: So, do you think I should bring my hair dryer with me?

Jamie: No, Sabrina, I don't think you'll need it in the jungle. Besides, the guide told us to

_____ [5] and bring essential items only.

Sabrina: Speaking of our travel guide, he seems really knowledgeable and practical. He's

very _____ [6]. I like his relaxed personality.

Jamie: Yes, so do I. I'm confident that we're _____ [7].
He's worked for the tour company for five years, and this is his third island excursion.

Sabrina: It's getting late. We really should _____ [8].
We have a big day ahead of us tomorrow. I'm so nervous that I won't be able to sleep.

Jamie: Relax, Sabrina. Try to _____ [9]. Everything will go as planned and will be

_____ [10]. We might even see giant turtles on our adventures!

Many young Canadians are volunteering their time in countries all over the world. For example, the Otesha Project is a Canadian youth organization that wants to change the way people treat our planet. *Otesha* means "reason to dream" in Swahili.

Another form of travel is increasing in popularity—volunteer travel or voluntourism. Some tourists volunteer in the communities they visit by working on projects like building homes or teaching. Learn about four Canadians featured in *Outpost Magazine* who have volunteered abroad.

Think of three volunteer jobs you could do in other countries before you read the article. Then describe the benefits of each volunteer job for you and the community.

Volunteer Job	Country	Benefits
Help teach in a rural elementary school	Ecuador	I could help improve the education of local children. I would learn another language and experience another culture.
1.		
2.		
3.		

Vocabulary

Match each word with its definition before you read. The line number is in parentheses.

1.	to train (v., 20)	**a.**	worth doing because it is important to you
2.	needs (n., 26)	**b.**	a method, way to do something
3.	a challenge (n., 31)	**c.**	to give the means, ability, or opportunity to do something
4.	rewarding (adj., 56)	**d.**	to be present and see something happen, like an accident
5.	a tool (n., 69)	**e.**	to teach someone new skills
6.	youth (n., 81)	**f.**	to make better
7.	to witness (v., 120)	**g.**	in a foreign country, usually on the other side of an ocean
8.	overseas (adv., 141)	**h.**	something new and difficult that demands a lot of effort
9.	to enable (v., 189)	**i.**	young people
10.	to improve (v., 194)	**j.**	requirements

Form a group of four students. Each of you should read a different volunteer profile. In the chart on page 59, fill in the section for the profile you read. Be prepared to talk about the information with the rest of the group.

Travellers for Change *Outpost Magazine*

More and more Canadians are volunteering to teach, provide medical aid, dig ditches, and build schools around the world. Get inspired by Travellers
5 for Change—four Canadians who build their lives around helping others in poor places all over the globe.

ZIMBABWE $53 000
Zoé Brabant — Nurse

Helping to the Limit
Zoé Brabant, 31 years old, nurse, Montréal,
10 Québec

Barely out of her third decade, Zoé Brabant has already participated in six missions with Médecins du Monde (MDM) in only four years, travelling to provide medical relief to
15 regions in crisis.

She was in Bam, Iran, following the devastating **earthquake** there in 2003, participated in the post-tsunami emergency efforts in Sri Lanka, and helped health care
20 centres in Afghanistan train local staff as part of that country's reconstruction. She has also served as a nurse in the remote villages of Ungava Bay in the north of Québec.

Brabant is currently serving in
25 Zimbabwe on an MDM mission to address the needs of orphans created by the AIDS pandemic. It's estimated that 25 per cent of the population has HIV.

Motivation
30 "I want to do my share on this small planet, to take up new challenges, and to learn more,

both personally and professionally. I want to discover new countries and new cultures. My mother has been a model for me. She
35 was a **midwife** in Québec and fought for women's rights to choose where they want to give birth. My mother has shown me that it is important to believe in the strength of what we can do."

40 **Frustrations**
"Injustice, suffering, poverty, and other humanitarian problems show us there are limits to what we can do. Addressing everything is impossible, particularly when
45 the needs are bigger than our resources. When there are few resources available, we sometimes have to forget individuals' problems to better address wider community problems."

Rewards
50 "To work abroad means leaving a lot behind, committing to other populations' needs, working in difficult conditions, and sometimes exposing ourselves to danger. However, it also means learning a lot, understanding the
55 planet better, and learning from others. Seeing the effect of our actions is always rewarding."

308 words

MAUREEN DOWDS
PHYSICAL EDUCATION
TEACHER
RWANDA
53 FRW

The Importance of Play
Maureen Dowds, 58 years old, physical-
60 education teacher and sport administrator, Winnipeg, Manitoba

A **retired** physical-education teacher, Maureen Dowds had already been closely involved with the Special Olympics before

⊳⊳

midwife (n.) → woman who helps mothers give birth

earthquake (n.) → shaking of the earth's surface, causing damage to buildings and people

retired (adj.) → no longer working, usually because of age

she joined Olympic Aid, now called Right
to Play (RTP), in 2001. RTP, founded
by Norwegian Olympic speed-skating
champion Johann Olav Koss, promotes
sport and play as important tools for child
development in the developing world.

It wasn't long after Dowds' initial
inquiry to RTP that she was on a plane
to establish the organization's first
programs in Ivory Coast and Angola,
followed by a two-year stint in Benin.
She's currently on assignment in Rwanda
on a joint RTP-UNICEF project to support
the implementation of a new physical-
education curriculum at the primary level.

Inspiration

"I have always loved my work with youth
and with children, especially those who
need a little extra support. I worked for
seven years teaching physical education to
adolescents with an intellectual disability,
and it was the best job I ever had—
they influenced me greatly. They share
themselves unconditionally."

On the Rwanda Project

"Most teachers in Rwanda have no
physical-education background, and they
come to teach **straight** out of high school.
Our program helps teachers understand
the value of structured play for kids. At
some schools, all children now participate
twice a day in games and activities.
Children who used to be isolated and **left
out** are now part of the whole. Children
with disabilities are being recognized and
accepted within their school community.
We hope this project will have a positive
effect on other schools."

Rewards

"Once, at a refugee camp in Benin,
work was being finished on a nearby
playground. It was one of the most exciting
days ever, to see the children's reactions
to the fresh cement being poured—they
had to be so patient. There were see-saws,
swings, monkey bars, geodesic domes for
climbing, a giant sandbox, and balance
blocks. That's my reward—seeing children
who have been through so much just
laughing and being children."

337 words

First in a Crisis

Jody Sydor, 37 years old, emergency-relief
coordinator, Vancouver, British Columbia

When Jody Sydor was a student at the
University of Victoria, she witnessed a
fatal car accident on the highway to the
Tsawwassen ferry. It would change the
course of her life.

"My first-aid training at the time,
while technically appropriate, still didn't
provide me with the confidence to act,"
Sydor says. She did what she could at
the scene, but immediately afterward
she immersed herself at the Canadian
Red Cross, eventually becoming a first-
aid instructor, then a trainer of first-aid
instructors.

Sydor's first international posting
with the Red Cross was in 1999, when
she went to Macedonia to supervise the
distribution of food and other essential
items to 225 000 refugees from Kosovo. In
May 2003, Sydor found herself in her first
war zone, in Iraq, where she conducted
rapid needs-assessments after the entry
of the coalition forces. When not overseas,
Sydor is the director of the North
Shore Emergency Management Office,
responsible for emergency planning
and preparedness for North and West
Vancouver.

What Is Emergency Management?

"It's about preparedness, response, and
recovery, which some say is a cyclical
process where you constantly prepare for
emergencies and learn from your actions.
It's the perfect field for people who are
problem-solvers with creative instincts,
combined with a sense of empathy or
compassion."

>>

straight (adv.) → directly

left out (adj.) → not allowed to
participate

playground (n.) → outdoor play
area with equipment like see-saws
and swings

recovery (n.) → return to a normal
condition

Frustrations

"The slow process of putting a strong aid program in place in a disaster zone and getting the recovery process underway is 160 frustrating. Disasters are, by definition, **overwhelming**. Typically, normal systems and services have been damaged or destroyed. It takes time."

Rewards

165 "I was in Indonesia for two months after the 2004 earthquake and tsunami. By the time I left to return home, we had emergency relief in place, and were starting the process of recovery. But in many locations, rebuilding 170 couldn't begin because bodies were still being recovered, leaving many people **displaced**. Recovery can't start until the emergency is over, but the emergency isn't over for a very long time. It requires patience 175 and perseverance."

343 words

Citizen Engineer

Paul Slomp, 25 years old, civil engineer, Rimbey, Alberta

180 Paul Slomp, only 25 years old, is already in his third year and third placement with Engineers Without Borders in Africa. He credits his parents with teaching him a sense of social responsibility early on. "My 185 parents were, and still are, global citizens," says Slomp.

He is currently working on an irrigation project with farmers in rural Zambia. The project's goal is to enable these farmers 190 to produce **crops** during the dry season, a time when they normally wouldn't be able to produce anything. "The crops produced under irrigation during this dry season," Slomp says, "can be used to improve the 195 family's food security and nutritional intake, or they can be sold to generate income for the family."

Motivation

"I look at the world today and see people 200 living on less than $1 per day, without access to safe drinking water and unable to meet their basic needs. But I also see a world full of wealth—people are living longer than ever before, and less effort 205 seems necessary to accomplish more. It seems unnecessary to have people living in poverty."

Frustrations

"Sometimes there's a gap in knowledge and 210 understanding between project designers and project implementers. Project designers can be so focused on increasing income and creating immediate international opportunities that they miss the local opportunities 215 that are often less risky and build the infrastructure and mentality for long-term export market gains."

Rewards

Slomp says that meeting people like John 220 Mwale, a 31-year-old farmer in a small village near Kampala, is a reward. Five years ago, Mwale was a subsistence farmer who hardly produced enough food for his family. Then he decided to learn more 225 about irrigation. He cleared a small plot of land to grow tomatoes and cabbage. He expanded this garden to two hectares and sold 5 000 heads of cabbage for $1 each during the first four months. Now he 230 shares his knowledge with the rest of the community.

334 words

The article "Travellers for Change" was originally published in Outpost Magazine *and* 235 *is reprinted in part with their permission.*

overwhelming (adj.) → too great to overcome

displaced (adj.) → without a home

crops (n.) → plants grown for food

Share information with the three classmates who read a different volunteer profile and fill in the rest of the chart together. To gather the required information, ask questions and give complete answers.

What is Zoé's occupation? She is a nurse. What motivates Zoé to volunteer? She likes the challenge.

	Helping to the Limit	The Importance of Play	First in a Crisis	Citizen Engineer
1. Name	Zoé Brabant	Maureen Dowds	Jody Sydor	Paul Slomp
2. Age				
3. Occupation				
4. Hometown				
5. Volunteer organization				
6. Goal of organization				
7. Countries where volunteered				
8. Motivation				
9. Frustrations				
10. Rewards				

Travel Quotes

Travelling the world has inspired many of the world's greatest minds.

Work with a partner and explain the meaning of each of the following travel quotes. Then decide if you agree or disagree with these messages about life, learning, and travel. Discuss your point of view with your partner.

The Quote	Meaning or Message	Do You Agree or Disagree? Explain
1. "Don't tell me how educated you are, tell me how much you travelled." Prophet Muhammad	Knowledge does not come from books or school but from seeing and experiencing the world.	
2. "Where we love is home—home that our feet may leave but not our hearts." Oliver Wendell Holmes		
3. "Twenty years from now you will be more disappointed by the things you didn't do than by the ones you did do. So throw off the bowlines, sail away from the safe harbour. Catch the trade winds in your sails. Explore. Dream. Discover." Mark Twain		
4. "If you reject the food, ignore the customs, fear the religion and avoid the people, you might better stay at home." James Michener		
5. "You have to risk going too far to discover just how far you can really go." T.S. Eliot		

◀◎▶ [WATCHING] One Couch at a Time

This documentary follows Alexandra Liss through her seven-month couchsurfing adventure and discusses the "age of sharing" we are entering. It pushes us to ask ourselves, "What would you be willing to share with a stranger?"

Vocabulary

Match each word with its correct definition before you watch.

1. a couch (n.)		**a.**	any person you do not know
2. meaningful (adj.)		**b.**	to be afraid of
3. to share (v.)		**c.**	people combining their money to support another person's project
4. a stranger (n.)		**d.**	to have or place confidence in
5. crowdfunding (n.)		**e.**	a sofa
6. to trust (v.)		**f.**	having great purpose
7. to fear (v.)		**g.**	money as a medium of exchange
8. currency (n.)		**h.**	to allow someone to use or enjoy something that you own

Comprehension

Read the questions. Then watch the video and answer them.

Introduction

1. Watch the introduction and check off all the countries mentioned. Can you locate all these countries on a map?

☐ Australia ☐ Canada ☐ Ireland ☐ Japan ☐ Thailand
☐ Botswana ☐ France ☐ Italy ☐ Morocco ☐ USA
☐ Brazil ☐ Germany ☐ Jamaica ☐ South Africa ☐ Zimbabwe

Couchsurfing Explained

2. Watch the next part of the video and circle T or F to indicate if the statement is true or false. If it is false, write the correct statement on the line.

   a. Casey Fenton is the creator of the couchsurfing website. **T** **F**

   _____

   b. Alexandra met Casey in 2006. T F

   _____

   c. Couchsurfing is a social-networking site. **T** **F**

   _____

   d. The purpose of couchsurfing is to offer a cheap way to travel. **T** **F**

   _____

e. Couchsurfing is dangerous, just like eBay.   T   F

_____

f. Alexandra wants everyone to know how couchsurfing can create better lives.   T   F

_____

g. She visited six continents and 25 countries.   **T**   **F**

_____

Couchsurfing in Rio De Janeiro, Brazil

3. Describe Marcelle and her apartment.

_____

_____

4. What is the goal of the couchsurfing "meet up" they go to?

_____

5. What is unique about the view from Ryan Fix's apartment window?

_____

6. According to Ryan, are we all the same? Explain what he says.

_____

_____

_____

7. What is "collaborative consumption"? Give some examples.

_____

_____

The Conclusion

8. Watch the conclusion of this documentary and summarize the main idea in your own words.

_____

_____

_____

_____

9. List three forms of sharing mentioned in the conclusion.

_____

_____

FYI

Did you know that you can exchange your home or your apartment with people from all over the world? Families or individuals who want to travel to another country and live for free post their home on one of the many house-swap websites. Then people from all over the world answer your request to trade homes. Sometimes a car, pets, bicycles, and even neighbourhood hospitality are included in the trade.

Discussion

1. From the list below, what would you be willing to share with a stranger? What would you not be willing to share? Explain your answer.

   ☐ Your couch ☐ Your car ☐ Your bike ☐ Your apartment ☐ Your job

   Other: _____

2. What are the positive and negative aspects of sharing our material goods?

3. Do you think collaborative consumption will become more or less popular in the near future? Why or why not?

4. Do you think couchsurfing is a good way to travel? What are the risks and rewards?

🗨 SPEAKING The Transforming Power of Travel

How does travel have the power to create lasting changes in our personality, our skills, and the way we see the world?

Work in small groups to fill in the chart. Discuss the important life lessons that the people in this unit learned from their travel adventures.

Person	Where Did They Go?	What Did They Do?	What Did They Learn?	What Did They Risk?
1. Rex Pemberton				
2. Tori Holmes				
3. Travellers for Change				
4. Alexandra Liss				
5. Add your name:	Where did/will you go?	What did/will you do?	What did/will you learn?	What did/will you risk?

Write a text or give an oral presentation on one of the following topics. Try to incorporate the elements seen in the unit from the Make the Connection box and use as many of the Top Words as you can, where appropriate.

Make the Connection

- ☐ The future
- ☐ Vocabulary and idioms from the unit
- ☐ Pronouncing the /*th*/ sound
- ☐ Getting meaning from context
- ☐ Descriptive writing

▶ Refer to Writing Files 2, page 65, for information on essays.

▶ Refer to appendix 1, page 155, for information on oral presentations.

1 TRAVEL ON THE EDGE: Why do so many people put themselves in dangerous situations when they travel? Refer to Rex Pemberton's and Tori Holmes' adventures, or another experience of travelling on the edge.

2 VOLUNTEER TRAVEL: Do you want to immerse yourself in a new culture and give back to society? Research an organization you could join that will help you reach your volunteering goals. Describe your volunteer intentions and the mission of the organization you selected.

> Canada World Youth   Québec Without Borders   Red Cross   Right to Play

3 COUCHSURFING: In which country would you like to couchsurf? Research the life and culture of one of the countries presented in the couchsurfing video or another country of your choice. Describe what you will do, see, and learn. How do you predict this adventure will change you?

4 WHAT'S MINE IS YOURS!: The collaborative consumption movement is considered one of the top 10 ideas that will change the world. Research one form of this sharing culture to learn about its positive and negative aspects. How will it affect the community where it is implemented?

> Car-sharing   Ride-sharing   Bike-sharing   Couchsurfing

5 TRAVEL LESSONS: What important life lesson(s) have you learned from travelling?

6 OTHER: _____ Write about another topic of your choice linked to what you learned in this unit. Make sure to have your topic approved by your teacher.

Top Words

Put a check mark next to the words you know and refer to the page numbers to learn the ones you don't know. Add to the list other words you want to remember from the unit.

ADJECTIVES
- ☐ **meaningful** (61)
- ☐ **rewarding** (55)

EXPRESSIONS
- ☐ **cut off from** (52)

ADVERBS
- ☐ **overseas** (55)

NOUNS
- ☐ **boundaries** (48)
- ☐ **dream** (48)
- ☐ **earth** (48)
- ☐ **minds** (48)
- ☐ **needs** (55)

- ☐ **overachiever** (51)
- ☐ **stranger** (61)
- ☐ **strength** (52)
- ☐ **tool** (55)
- ☐ **youth** (55)

VERBS
- ☐ **to climb** (48)
- ☐ **to enable** (55)
- ☐ **to fear** (61)
- ☐ **to improve** (55)
- ☐ **to share** (61)
- ☐ **to trust** (61)

OTHER:

_____   _____

_____   _____

Vocabulary from the unit and other theme-related vocabulary can be practised online.

The Essay

Model Essay

An essay is a short piece of writing on a particular topic. It is often written from the author's point of view. The word *essay* is derived from the French word *essayer*, which means *to try*. An essay is an attempt to express your point of view on a topic.

An essay is made up of **three** types of paragraphs:

1. The **introduction** engages the reader's interest and contains an attention-getter and a thesis statement.

   ▶ The **attention-getter** is an opening sentence that grabs the readers' attention and encourages them to read the essay.

   ▶ The **thesis statement** clearly indicates the central idea of the essay and the main ideas that will be developed.

2. Each **body paragraph** focuses on one of the main ideas described in the thesis statement.

   ▶ The **topic sentence** of each body paragraph supports the thesis statement.

3. The **conclusion** summarizes the main ideas of the essay and brings it to an interesting close.

Practice 1

Study the following model essay. Highlight the thesis statement and underline the topic sentences.

Did you know that about half of all Canadian households own at least one pet? That means an astounding 25.5 million domestic animals: eight million cats, six million dogs, and more than eleven million birds, fish, and reptiles. Feeding and caring for these animals has a huge impact on the environment—and the economy.

Both the food that pets eat, and the waste they produce, pose problems. Canadians buy more than a half-million tonnes of cat and dog food every year and environmentalists are starting to worry about the impact of producing this food—the fossil fuel, fertilizer, pesticides, water, and machinery used to grow, package, and transport it. When the mountain of waste pets produce—620 000 tonnes a year by dogs alone—is added, the pressure on the earth is enormous. Domestic animals are given far more food than they need, and much of this is protein that comes from fish, lamb, and beef. All of these food sources make a significant contribution to the environmental footprint.

Pet supporters are quick to argue that the pet industry provides jobs and helps the economy, and this is true, but at what cost? Ecologists in New Zealand discovered that the environmental cost of owning a pet is comparable to the making and running of a car. Owning a medium-sized dog is twice as environmentally expensive as making a Toyota Land Cruiser and driving it for a year (10 000 kilometres). Cats are about one-fifth as needy, roughly equal to doing the same with a Volkswagen Golf.

▷

Then there are pet health-care costs. Insurance companies in the United States pay out $34-million annually for claims to cover weight-related illnesses such as dog diabetes and cat asthma.

No one wants to stop people owning a beloved cat or dog—or even a fish or a reptile. Perhaps pet owners need to use a little more common sense, though. As David MacKay, chief science adviser to Britain's Energy and Climate Change Department, advised: "We should pick pets like we pick cars—the smaller and fewer, the better."

The Thesis Statement

A thesis statement is a sentence that states the central idea of your essay and indicates the main points you will develop.

A thesis statement should:	A thesis statement should not be:
• Express a point of view, attitude, or opinion about a topic • Be a statement for which you can develop support • Have a controlling idea that focuses your essay • Contain the main points to be explored	• A personal expression ▶ ~~I will talk about the advantages of travel.~~ (no main points) • A question ▶ ~~Are boys more romantic than girls?~~ (no point of view) • An obvious fact ▶ ~~Fifty per cent of marriages end in divorce.~~ (no point of view) • Too broad ▶ ~~Many people like to travel.~~ (not specific enough) • Too narrow ▶ ~~Some people like to go to the movies on a first date.~~ (too limited to develop into a whole essay)

To write a thesis statement, combine your topic and main points. Here is a simple formula for constructing effective thesis statements:

Topic	Link	Main Point 1	Main Point 2
Being in love	has	positive effects on your health	and happiness.
Couchsurfing	teaches people	tolerance	and trust.

Practice 2

Circle the topic, underline the link, and double underline the main points in each of the thesis statements below.

Example: (The essential features of a good relationship) are honesty, communication, and respect.

1. Bike-sharing, ride-sharing and co-working will help create a greener future.

2. Fad diets are expensive, ineffective, and even dangerous to your health.

3. Students who combine a full-time job with a full-time program face problems at school, work, and home.

4. Money problems, the death of a family member, and a new job are the three major causes of stress.

Explain why these thesis statements are not effective.

1. In my essay, I will talk about love. _____

2. Why do people travel? _____

3. Everybody should ride-share every day. _____

4. Eighty-five per cent of girls dream of getting married someday. _____

Write It!

Write a thesis statement for one of these topics on a separate piece of paper. Make sure to include two main points in your thesis statement.

> couchsurfing   Facebook   love in other cultures   pets   siblings   travelling   smartphones
>
> other: _____

The Difference Between a Thesis Statement and a Topic Sentence

Refer to Writing Files 1, page 21, for more information on topic sentences.

An essay has one **thesis statement**, which is found in the introduction. It explains what the essay is about.

Each body paragraph has one **topic sentence**. It explains what the paragraph is about.

The main points in your thesis statement become the focuses of your topic sentences.

Thesis statement: *To reduce traffic congestion and noise pollution in major urban centres, more people should use bike share programs.*

Topic sentence 1: Traffic congestion	Topic sentence 2: Noise pollution
If more people biked to work or school every day, there would be fewer cars on the road.	Biking is quiet, unlike car traffic.

Practice 4

Read the following thesis statement and then write three topic sentences to support it.

Thesis statement: *Students who combine a full-time job with a full-time program face problems at school, work, and home.*

Topic sentence 1: Problems at school	Topic sentence 2: Problems at work	Topic sentence 3: Problems at home

Write two topic sentences on a separate piece of paper to accompany the thesis statement you wrote in the Write It! on page 67.

The Essay Outline

An outline is a plan or map of your essay from beginning to end. It helps you plan what you want to say about each main point before you begin to write.

Practice 5

Create a detailed outline for the model essay on page 65.

Introduction	Attention-getter		_____
	Thesis statement		_____
Development (body paragraphs)	**Paragraph 1**	Topic sentence	_____
		Support 1	_____
		Support 2	_____
		Support 3	_____
	Paragraph 2	Topic sentence	_____
		Support 1	_____
		Support 2	_____
		Support 3	_____
Conclusion	Summary		_____
	Memorable statement		_____

Create an essay outline on a separate piece of paper using the topic of the thesis statement from the Write It! on page 67. Make sure to develop your outline using the topic sentences from the Write It! on page 68.

Refer to Writing Files 1, page 21, for more information on paragraphs, topic sentences, and supporting ideas.

Write It!

When you have crafted your thesis statement and created your essay outline, write your essay on a separate piece of paper. Your essay should be about 350 words long and contain four paragraphs.

Refer to Writing Files 3, page 109, for more information on introductions and conclusions.

Revising and Editing

When you revise an essay, you reread it to make sure that all of the ideas are clear, connected, and well organized. Then you edit it by checking for mistakes and correcting them. Use the checklists at the back of the book to help you.

Revise and Edit It!

Revise and edit the student's essay below.

1. Read the essay carefully and answer the questions about essay style and organization that follow each part.

2. Then reread the essay and find and correct 14 language errors (six verb errors, four singular/plural noun errors, four spelling errors). Underline each error and write the correction above it.

Introduction

Did you know that almost 80 percent of college students have part-time jobs? If you are one of them, then you know that many teacher and parents disagree with this life choice, claiming that these jobs take up too much time. However, college students gain a lot from having part-time jobs. It's important for a students to work because it develop their sense of responsibility and helps them to manage their time.

1. Does this introduction contain an effective attention-getter? Explain your answer.

2. Is the thesis statement clear and focused? Explain your answer.

3. What is the subject of this essay?

4. What two points do you expect to be explained in this essay?

Paragraph 1

Firstly, a part-time job teaches students how to be responsible. They begin to understand that we have to work to make money to be able to buy what we want or need. Many student have to pay for their own apartment, food, and smartphone, so they need to work to pay the bills. Part-time jobs also teach students to be ponctuel and to respect the rules in the work environnment. If they arrive late, they could be fired. If they are impolite to customers, they will be severely reprimanded. Work teaches students about real-life consequences. In short, students acquire qualities and qualifications from part-time jobs that they doesn't learn in the classroom.

1. Does this paragraph contain a clear topic sentence? If so, highlight it.
2. Does the author support or prove her topic sentence? _____
3. Sentence 2 is confusing. Can you improve it? Who is the author referring to? _____
_____

Paragraph 2

Secondly, working part-time helps students to learn how to manage their time carefuly. It was not until I started working 20 hours a week at a coffee shop that I have learned how to use the agenda on my smartphone. Now I plan and schedule my courses, my homeworks, my work shifts, and my social activities at the beginning of every week. Having good time-management skills gonna help students to succeed in their futur careers.

1. Does this paragraph contain a clear topic sentence? If so, highlight it.
2. Does the author support or prove the topic sentence? _____

Conclusion

To sum up, part-time jobs teaches students essential life skills such as responsibility and time management that cannot be learned in the classroom. Society should not to discourage students from working while at college. Instead, it should reward them. What kind of society would we live in if students didn't work?

1. Highlight the summary. Does it summarize the main points of the essay? _____
2. Does the conclusion end with a memorable statement or question? _____

Write It!

Use the checklists at the back of the book to revise and edit your own essay or a classmate's.

RELATIONSHIPS

Does Love Make the World Go Around?

The science and culture of relationships

> Have you ever wondered why or how you fall in love?

> How has online technology changed the way we meet and interact?

> What type of relationship personality do you have?

> How is love portrayed in other cultures?

In this unit, you will explore the scientific, technological, and cultural aspects of love and relationships.

LOVE AT FIRST SIGHT

Relationship Quiz

What factors are important when you choose your ideal partner?

Rate the following factors on a scale of 1 (not important) to 5 (very important) and answer the questions.

scent (n) → a pleasant smell

Factor 1: Physical Appearance

1   2   3   4   5

What physical attributes attract you?

_____
_____
_____
_____
_____

Factor 4: Scent

1   2   3   4   5

Animals rely on their sense of smell to find a mate. Do you?

_____
_____
_____
_____
_____

Factor 2: Personality

1   2   3   4   5

What personality traits are important to you? Describe them.

_____
_____
_____
_____
_____

Factor 5: Financial Status

1   2   3   4   5

Are you more attracted to someone who has money and a job? Explain your answer.

_____
_____
_____
_____
_____

Factor 3: Mutual Interests

1   2   3   4   5

Do you tend to fall in love with someone who shares your interests? Explain your answer.

_____
_____
_____
_____

Factor 6: Commitment

1   2   3   4   5

Are you looking for someone who you could be with long term? Explain your answer.

_____
_____
_____
_____

Grammar Link

QUESTION FORMATION

Use the auxiliary *do/does* for questions in the simple present and *did* for questions in the simple past.

(Question word) + auxiliary verb + subject + base form of the main verb (QWASV)

*How **do** you **fall** in love?*

*What **did** she **look** like?*

Exception: Do not use an auxiliary with the verb *be*.

*What physical characteristics **are** important to you?*

▶ Refer to *REAL Grammar Book 2, appendix 2.*

Interview two classmates. Ask them to explain their answers to the survey questions. Write their number ratings and summarize their answers in the chart. Ask accurate questions and give complete answers. Refer to the Grammar Link on question formation for help.

	Rating	Student 1	Rating	Student 2
1. Physical appearance				
2. Personality				
3. Mutual interests				
4. Scent				
5. Financial status				
6. Commitment				

Writing

Summarize the data you collected from your classmates. Which factors appear to be the most important?

_____

_____

_____

How To

ACTIVATE PRIOR KNOWLEDGE

The more you know about a topic, the better you will understand the text.

To activate prior knowledge:

- Predict what the text may be about based on the title and illustration.
- Take some time to think about and discuss what you know about the subject.
- Record your ideas.

Do you know why you are attracted to a certain person? Scientific research reveals some answers.

Discuss the following questions with a partner to find out what you already know. Write down your thoughts in point form in the first column of the chart.

	Your Initial Thoughts	What the Article Says
1. Why do opposites attract?		
2. Do looks matter more to men or women?		
3. Is love blind?		
4. Can love be a drug?		
5. Is love good for your health?		
6. Why do people cheat?		
7. What keeps people together in a long-term relationship?		

Vocabulary

Match each word or expression with its correct definition before you read. The line number is in parentheses.

1.	an attraction (n., 10)		**a.**	to promise to stay with someone
2.	looks (n., 30)		**b.**	a mutual force pulling two objects or people together
3.	to cheat (v., 39)		**c.**	to hug or embrace fondly
4.	blind (adj., 56)		**d.**	the state of a person's body or mind
5.	to be aware (v., 59)		**e.**	physical appearance, especially when pleasing
6.	health (n., 91)		**f.**	to be unfaithful to your partner
7.	to commit (v., 119)		**g.**	unable to see
8.	to cuddle (v., 123)		**h.**	to know or understand

Read the article. Then return to the chart and fill in the second column, based on the information in the article. Discuss with your partner whether your initial thoughts match what the article says.

Listen to "On Desire" online to learn more about the science of love and attraction.

The Mysteries of Love From the pages of *Real Simple*

Why does love hit you so hard? And why does one handsome stranger make your heart pound while another leaves you cold? Love has always been a
5 mystery. But researchers now have some explanations—many based on sophisticated brain-scanning techniques—that shed light on how it works. Here are some questions about love, partially demystified.

10 **What rules attraction?**
In general, you gravitate toward people like you. Good-looking people tend to go for similarly good-looking types, and those from a particular socio-economic
15 background favour their own. Experts believe this happens because perceived equality contributes to a stable union.

But once you get past the bone structure and bank account and into personality
20 attributes, opposites often attract. "We're apt to fall in love with those who are mysterious and challenging to us," says Helen Fisher, a professor of anthropology at Rutgers and the author of *Why We Love*.
25 "This pull to another biological type could also be adaptive. If two very different people

pool their DNA, they'll create more genetic variety, and their young will come to the job of parenting with a wider **array** of skills."

30 **How much do looks count?**
Physical features are important to both sexes, but a bit more so to men.

"During attraction, the parts of a man's brain associated with processing
35 visual information are more active," says Louann Brizendine of the University of California at San Francisco and the author of *The Female Brain*.

Why do people cheat?
40 Attraction, romantic love, and attachment involve three overlapping but separate brain systems. "It's not hard for somebody to sexually desire one person, be infatuated with another, and still want to spend the rest
45 of his or her life with a third," says Fisher. Because each kind of love serves a unique need and exists in a different context, cheaters are able to divide their emotional resources. Fisher suspects the propensity
50 to **stray** may be stronger in people who

array (n.) → variety

stray (v.) → cheat

>>

novelty-seeking (adj.) → always looking for something new and different

have **novelty-seeking**, dopamine-sensitive personalities. But factors unique to the relationship—a need for attention, a desire to get out of the situation—are just as likely
55 to fuel infidelity.

Is love blind?

Not exactly, but once you're hooked, your vision gets **cloudy**. "When you're in a relationship, you're aware of the other
60 person's **flaws**, but your brain is telling you it's OK to ignore them," says Lucy Brown, a professor of neuroscience at the Albert Einstein College of Medicine, who specializes in the brain's response to love.

65   According to Fisher, this mechanism may have evolved to help people **stick** together through early, sometimes stressful, child-rearing stages.

Can love be addictive?

70 Love **plays havoc with** your body chemistry, causing you to act like an addict bent on scoring her next fix. Studies have found that serotonin levels decrease by up to 40 per cent in the newly **smitten**, causing some to show
75 signs of obsessive-compulsive disorder. Also, cortisol, a stress hormone linked with the fight-or-flight response, is released, so you're constantly on high alert. Sound familiar?

    Research by a team that included
80 Brown and Fisher found that people who had recently fallen in love showed strong activity in the area of the brain that produces and receives dopamine, a neurotransmitter associated with addictive behaviour whose
85 activity increases when you expect to receive a reward. "You're not supposed to be satisfied," explains Fisher. "You're supposed to be driven so that you can win the person and eventually stabilize your internal
90 chemistry."

Can love affect your health?

Research has found that couples in good relationships tend to be healthier and happier. "Happily married couples report
95 lower stress than single people, in part because they provide each other with emotional support in difficult times," says Janice Kiecolt-Glaser of Ohio State University. "Lower stress translates to better
100 health and immune function."

What keeps people together?

Hormones and hard work. **Restlessness** sets in one to two years into a relationship, according to new research from the
105 universities of Pavia and Pisa, in Italy. That's the period in which the chemical activity associated with new love (high dopamine, for example) dies down.

    Fortunately, there are ways to keep
110 the spark alive. Sexual contact drives up dopamine levels. Novelty does, too, which is why you tend to feel so good about somebody after taking a trip or going through an unusual experience together. Frequent physical
115 contact is most likely to maintain elevated oxytocin levels, which is why holding hands, stroking your partner, or any other kind of touch can create feelings of attachment.

What makes people commit?

120 Humans are hard-wired to stick together. Intimate relationships trigger the production of oxytocin and vasopressin, chemicals that scientists have nicknamed "cuddle hormones."

    A mere touch from a loved one can
125 elevate their levels, and after sex they flood the system.

    These hormones play an important role later on in the relationship, Brown says, "when you really know the person's flaws."

809 words

cloudy (adj.) → unfocused

flaws (n.) → bad qualities

restlessness (n.) → impatience

stick (v.) → stay or remain

plays havoc with (exp.) → upsets

smitten (adj.) → infatuated

▶ Refer to Grammar Link, page 73, for more information on question formation.

Focus on Language: Question Formation

1. Study the form of the eight questions in the subtitles of the article you just read. For each question:

    a. Underline the question word if there is one.   **c.** Draw a square around the subject.

    b. Circle the auxiliary if there is one.   **d.** Highlight the main verb.

2. When do you not use an auxiliary in English questions?

_____

3. How is *be* different from other verbs in question formation?

_____

Opinion Poll

Do you and your classmates hold similar views on dating? The following opinion poll will help you find out.

Answer the following questions. Use the modal *should* to give your opinion. Then ask two of your classmates what they think. Be sure to support and explain your point of view.

	Your Answer	Student 1	Student 2
1. What is the best way to meet people you might like to date? Why?			
2. Who should invite the other person to go on the first date? Why?			
3. Who should pay on the first date? Why?			
4. Where should you go on the first date? Why?			
5. When should you introduce your partner to your parents?			
6. Should you date someone you meet online? Why or why not?			

How To

GIVE YOUR OPINION USING *SHOULD*

The modal *should* is commonly used for opinions, advice, and recommendations.

You **should** *go on the roller coaster at La Ronde on your first date.*

Should *I wear these new jeans to the concert?*

FYI

Why are you always thinking about your boyfriend or girlfriend? It's natural! Scientists say that the chemical profile of people in love is similar to that of people with a mental illness such as obsessive-compulsive disorder.

 **WATCHING** # When Strangers Click

In the following documentary, you will explore the idea of meeting someone and falling in love in the virtual world.

Discussion

1. Do you play realistic video games? Which ones? What does your "video game personality" look like?

2. Have you ever dated someone virtually or have you dated someone in person that you met in a virtual world?

3. What are the advantages of using an online dating service to meet someone? What are the disadvantages?

Vocabulary

Fill in the blanks below with words from the box before you watch. Check your answers as you watch the video.

dating
shallow
to get blinded by
to hit it off
to take my mind off
wedding

1. I was looking for something to _____ my problems.

2. The first time we met, we got along well together. We really _____.

3. _____ in Second Life is much different than real life because you can go anywhere and do anything you want.

4. I think that the advantage is that you don't _____ the

    _____ things like looks.

5. We decided to get a Second Life _____. It took a month of planning to get married and about 500 dollars.

Comprehension

Read the questions. Then watch the documentary and answer them.

1. Why did Jonas originally go online?

    _____

2. What is Second Life? Circle all the correct answers.
    a. It is a virtual world game.
    b. It allows you to be whatever you want to be.
    c. It is a place where people go to become famous.
    d. It is an online dating site.
    e. It is a virtual world built by its users.
    f. It happens in virtual time.

3. How did Nickel and Bara meet in Second Life? What was her impression of him?

    _____

    _____

Read "Online Dating and the Search for True Love - or Loves" online to learn how online dating is changing the way we find love.

4. How do you buy items in Second Life?

_____

_____

5. How is dating in Second Life easier than in the real world? Name some activities Bara and Nickel did together.

_____

_____

6. According to Beth and Jonas, what role does appearance, or the way you look, play in Second Life? Do you see anything ironic or strange about what they say?

_____

_____

_____

_____

7. How did Jonas and Beth meet in real life? What was her impression of him?

_____

_____

8. How does Jonas see his baby and "wife" every day?

_____

9. How did Jonas and Beth's "second life" positively affect their real life? Circle all the correct answers.

    a. They have a great child.   **d.** They have a legal marriage.

    b. Jonas did over 300 live shows.   **e.** They found real love.

    c. Jonas has a record deal.   **f.** They plan to live together in the real world soon.

Discussion and Writing

1. What do you think about Jonas and Beth's virtual relationship? Explain your answer.

2. Do you think the line between virtual and real relationships is becoming blurred? Explain your answer.

3. What are the advantages and disadvantages to having friendships or relationships in the virtual world?

Fill in the following chart with your ideas.

Advantages	Disadvantages

What is your relationship personality? According to anthropologist Helen Fisher, there are four different personality types. Discovering yours could help you find a good match.

Take the quiz to find out your personality type before you read the text on pages 82–83. Score your results using the blue box below.

1. I find unpredictable situations exciting.
- ☐ I strongly disagree
- ☐ I disagree
- ☐ I agree
- ☐ I strongly agree

2. I do things without planning in advance.
- ☐ I strongly disagree
- ☐ I disagree
- ☐ I agree
- ☐ I strongly agree

3. I always think of new ideas.
- ☐ I strongly disagree
- ☐ I disagree
- ☐ I agree
- ☐ I strongly agree

4. I have many different interests.
- ☐ I strongly disagree
- ☐ I disagree
- ☐ I agree
- ☐ I strongly agree

Total 1–4: _____

5. I make plans for the future.
- ☐ I strongly disagree
- ☐ I disagree
- ☐ I agree
- ☐ I strongly agree

6. I place a lot of importance on how other people view me.
- ☐ I strongly disagree
- ☐ I disagree
- ☐ I agree
- ☐ I strongly agree

7. I think it is important to follow the rules.
- ☐ I strongly disagree
- ☐ I disagree
- ☐ I agree
- ☐ I strongly agree

8. I am usually cautious, but not fearful.
- ☐ I strongly disagree
- ☐ I disagree
- ☐ I agree
- ☐ I strongly agree

Total 5–8: _____

9. I can see many different ways to solve a particular problem.
- ☐ I strongly disagree
- ☐ I disagree
- ☐ I agree
- ☐ I strongly agree

10. I am more intuitive than most people.
- ☐ I strongly disagree
- ☐ I disagree
- ☐ I agree
- ☐ I strongly agree

11. I change my way of thinking easily.
- ☐ I strongly disagree
- ☐ I disagree
- ☐ I agree
- ☐ I strongly agree

12. I get uncomfortable when I see someone standing alone at a party.
- ☐ I strongly disagree
- ☐ I disagree
- ☐ I agree
- ☐ I strongly agree

Total 9–12: _____

13. I am very focused.
- ☐ I strongly disagree
- ☐ I disagree
- ☐ I agree
- ☐ I strongly agree

14. I think it is more important to do a good job than to have people like me.
- ☐ I strongly disagree
- ☐ I disagree
- ☐ I agree
- ☐ I strongly agree

15. It takes a lot of evidence to make me change my way of thinking on most issues.
- ☐ I strongly disagree
- ☐ I disagree
- ☐ I agree
- ☐ I strongly agree

16. I am uncomfortable with uncertainties and prefer to clear them up quickly.
- ☐ I strongly disagree
- ☐ I disagree
- ☐ I agree
- ☐ I strongly agree

Total 13–16: _____

Give yourself points for each answer

Strongly disagree	**1 pt**
Disagree	**2 pts**
Agree	**3 pts**
Strongly agree	**4 pts**

Add up the number of points in each of the four sections: **1–4; 5–8; 9–12; 13–16.**
The two highest numbers are your primary and secondary types.
Questions 1–4 measure the degree to which you are an **explorer**.
Questions 5–8 measure the degree to which you are a **builder**.
Questions 9–12 measure the degree to which you are a **negotiator**.
Questions 13–16 measure the degree to which you are a **director**.

Vocabulary

Put a check mark beside the adjectives that describe you. Write **P** beside positive attributes and **N** beside negative attributes. Use a dictionary for help. Knowing these words will help you understand the text you will read.

✓ P	analytical	devoted	people-oriented
	annoying	distant	playful
	autonomous	fearful	restless
	bold	friendly	rude
	bragging	hardworking	sensuous
	captivating	ingenious	stubborn
	cautious	intuitive	successful
	dedicated	invasive	theoretical
	dependable	novelty-seeking	unpredictable

Grammar Link

ADJECTIVES

Adjectives describe and modify nouns. They can come before a noun.
*I like to date **dependable** people.*

They can follow the verb *be*.
*My girlfriend **is hardworking**.*

Adjectives do not agree in number with the noun.
*They are **bolds** and **unpredictables**.*

▷ Refer to *REAL Grammar Book 2,* unit 6.

Read the section of the text on pages 82–83 that corresponds to the personality type from your quiz results. Fill out the column in the chart for your personality type. Be sure to use your own words as much as possible. Then find three classmates that represent the other personality types and ask them for the information to complete the chart.

	Negotiator	Explorer	Director	Builder
Chemical system				
Positive personality traits				
Personality weaknesses				

Love Types

By Dr. Helen Fisher

handling (n.) → dealing with

weaknesses (n.) → personal defects or failings

wishy-washy (adj.) → indecisive

spinelessness (n.) → lack of courage

backstabbing (n.) → attacking (someone) unfairly, in a deceitful manner

on the spur of the moment (exp.) → with spontaneity

restless (adj.) → not able to relax

strive (v.) → make a great effort

core (adj.) → main

The Negotiator

Negotiators have specific personality traits that have been linked to estrogen. Although estrogen is known as a female sex hormone, men have it, too, and there are plenty of male Negotiators. This type is good at **handling** people. Negotiators instinctively know what others
5 are thinking and feeling. They artfully read facial expressions, postures, gestures, and tone of voice. They are introspective and self-analytical—men and women who take pleasure in journeying into their thoughts and motives. As a result, when they form a partnership, they like to continually analyze the strengths and **weaknesses** of the relationship.

Negotiators are flexible. They tend to be comfortable with ambiguity. Negotiators can be
10 highly intuitive and creative. And they like to theorize. Perhaps their most distinctive characteristic is verbal fluency, the facility for finding the right words rapidly. With this skill—alongside an agreeable and accommodating nature, compassion, social awareness, and patience—the Negotiator can be very friendly, diplomatic, and authentic.

But as with all qualities, these traits can become problematic. Negotiators, with their desire
15 to please everyone, can sometimes appear **wishy-washy** to the point of **spinelessness**. Because they're not willing to confront, they can turn to **backstabbing**. With their need to examine all the possibilities, they can be slow to react. And in a relationship, their desire to connect and dissect all the subtle meanings between the two of you can become annoying and invasive.

The Explorer

20 Explorers have a very active dopamine system, a brain chemical associated with the tendency to seek novelty, among other qualities. An Explorer might look up from the newspaper on Sunday and say, "Want to go to Warsaw?"—and by Wednesday you're in Poland. Champions of "never a dull moment," these adventurers live to discover new people, places, things, or ideas, often **on the spur of the moment**. Friends, family, and colleagues frequently regard them as highly independent and
25 autonomous.

Explorers have more energy than most people; they tend to be **restless**, sometimes fast-paced. And they are highly curious—"For always roaming with a hungry heart," as the poet Tennyson put it. Constantly generating new ideas or creative insights, they easily shift their attention from one thing to another.

30 People quickly like most Explorers. Generous and sunny, they tend to be playful, sensual, often unpredictable, and regularly amusing. But they can be difficult to live with, especially in a marriage. They do not tolerate boredom well, so they are generally not interested in routine social or business events. In fact, Explorers try to avoid routine of almost any kind, and can step on another person's cherished beliefs and habits. They are also impatient.

35 ### The Director

Specific activities in the testosterone system are what distinguish this type. Again, although we think of the hormone as male, it is shared by both sexes. Whatever the gender, people of this type are competitive. They **strive** to be on top and have many skills to get there. They are pragmatic, decisive, and able to make up their minds rapidly, even when faced with difficult choices. Rational
40 analysis, logical reasoning, and objectivity are their **core** strengths. They also pay attention to details and can focus their attention to the exclusion of everything around them. Many Directors are also ingenious, theoretical, and bold in their ideas. Moreover, they are willing to take unpopular, even dangerous paths, to get to the truth. So they persist and often win.

Directors are particularly skilled at understanding machines and other rule-based systems,
45 from computers and math problems to the details of biology, world finance, or architecture. They excel at sports, and often have an ear for music. Their interests can be narrow, but they pursue them deeply and thoroughly. And they can captivate those who share their hobbies.

Directors often choose to do a good job rather than please others. In fact, they are the least socially skilled of the four types. When preoccupied with work or personal goals, they can appear distant, even cold, and are generally not interested in making social connections, with the exception of those that are useful or exciting to them.

As with the other types, the traits that make Directors so successful may become problematic. For example, their confidence can turn into bragging, their exactitude can turn uncompromising, and their **forthrightness** can simply seem **rude**. And because they often see issues in black and white, they miss the nuances of social, business, and personal situations. But thanks to their dedication, loyalty, and interest in sharing ideas, Directors make close friends. And they can be fiercely protective of those they love.

The Builder

Calm, affable, and people-oriented, the Builder's personality is influenced by the serotonin system. Social situations are often fun and relaxing for Builders. They like to network. Because duty and loyalty are their **strong suits**, they often have a devoted group of friends. And they're true guardians when it comes to family and friends.

Builders are cautious but not **fearful**. They think concretely. They have a clear memory of past mistakes, so they prepare. These people are not impulsive with their money, their actions, or their feelings. Security is important to them. Structure and order are, too. Many are traditional, and they often have strong morals. Builders don't **get bored** easily, which enables them to be methodical, hardworking, and dependable.

But Builders can go too far in their **quest** to do things the "proper way." They can be intolerant of other ways. Indeed, they can be **stubborn** and with their need for order, rules, and schedules, they can lack spontaneity. Their stoicism can turn into pessimism, their conformity into rigidity, and their concrete thinking sometimes makes them too literal. Normally, however, Builders are community minded, industrious, and popular with colleagues and companions.

945 words

forthrightness (n.) → direct, outspoken manner

rude (adj.) → impolite

strong suits (exp.) → strong points

fearful (adj.) → afraid

get bored (exp.) → lose interest

quest (n.) → adventure

stubborn (adj.) → resistant

Pronunciation

Word Stress

English is a stress-timed language. This means that, in words of two or more syllables, one syllable receives more emphasis than the others. For example, in the word *marriage*, the first syllable is pronounced more strongly: **mar**·riage.

Listen carefully to the pronunciation of these words heard in the video on the next page. Underline the stressed syllable. Then repeat these words aloud. Remember to put the emphasis on the correct syllable.

1. pho·to·graph
2. po·ten·tial
3. ex·peri·ence
4. so·ci·e·ty
5. de·sire
6. ex·treme
7. ed·u·cat·ed
8. tra·di·tion·al
9. rev·o·lu·tion
10. re·bel·lion
11. ro·mance
12. di·vorce
13. re·al·i·ty
14. cul·tures
15. pov·er·ty

In this *National Geographic* photo-documentary, Jodi Cobb discusses how she tried to capture how people define love around the world. It's not all hearts and flowers!

FYI

How many people do you think you should date before you settle down? Some researchers say a dozen. Their research indicates that when it comes to picking a partner, people are most successful if they have already had 12 relationship experiences, no matter how brief.

Discussion

1. With a 50 per cent divorce rate in North America, should people still get married? Explain your answer.

2. Why do you think the divorce rate is so high?

3. In some cultures, marriages are arranged. What are the advantages and disadvantages of arranged marriages?

Comprehension

Watch the photo-documentary and take detailed notes. Use the headings and boxes to guide your note-taking.

The Stages of Love

Lust	Romantic Love	Attachment

The Downside of Love

In India	In Taiwan	In Japan

Use your notes to determine if the following statement is true or false. If it is false, write the correct statement on the line provided. Then watch the photo-documentary again to check your answers.

1. Jodi Cobb finds the task of photographing love easy.   T   F

   _____

2. Men are attracted to women with a desirable waist-to-hip ratio.   T   F

   _____

3. Romantic love lasts about four years because this is the amount of time needed for a baby to be "viable."   T   F

   _____

4. The chemical responsible for attachment is oxytocin.   T   F

   _____

5. In India they say first comes love, then comes marriage.   T   F

   _____

6. The practice of child weddings is widely accepted by all in India.   T   F

   _____

7. In India, a woman without a man has no status in society.   T   F

   _____

8. Taiwanese men prefer the aggressive, assertive nature of the Chinese women.   T   F

   _____

READING   FOR CHALLENGE

What would you be willing to do to make someone fall in love with you? This short story describes what the main character is willing to do for true love.

Vocabulary

Find words or expressions in the text that are similar in meaning to the following words. The line number is given in parentheses.

FYI

In 1960, the popular American television series *The Twilight Zone* based one of its episodes on John Collier's "The Chaser" (pictured on the next page).

1.	looked around (3)		5.	contempt or disdain (60)	
2.	small (7)		6.	to like (65)	
3.	expensive (44)		7.	appreciative (107)	
4.	to last forever (54)		8.	to be richer (110)	

The Chaser
By John Collier

Alan Austen, as nervous as a kitten, went up dark and creaky stairs in the neighbourhood of Pell Street, and peered about for a long time on the **dim landing** before he found the name he wanted written obscurely on
5 one of the doors. **1**

He pushed open this door, as he had been told to do, and found himself in a tiny room, which contained little furniture—a plain kitchen table, a rocking-chair, and an ordinary chair. On one of the dirty beige walls were a couple
10 of shelves, containing in all perhaps a dozen bottles and jars. **2**

An old man sat in the rocking-chair, reading a newspaper. Alan, without a word, handed him the card he had been given. "Sit down, Mr. Austen," said the old man very politely. "I am glad to meet you. **3**
15 "Is it true," asked Alan, "that you have a mixture that has—quite extraordinary effects?" **4**

"My dear sir," replied the old man, "my stock is not very large but, it is varied. I think nothing I sell has effects which could be precisely described as ordinary." **5**
20 "Well, the fact is. . ." began Alan. **6**

"Here, for example," interrupted the old man, reaching for a bottle from the shelf. "Here is a liquid as colourless as water, almost tasteless, quite imperceptible in coffee, wine, or any other beverage. It is also quite imperceptible to any known
25 method of autopsy." **7**

"Do you mean it is a poison?" cried Alan, very much horrified. **8**

"Call it a glove cleaner if you like," said the old man indifferently. "Maybe it will clean gloves. I have never tried.
30 One might call it a life cleaner. Lives need cleaning sometimes." **9**

"I want nothing of that sort," said Alan. **10**

"Probably it is just as well," said the old man. "Do you **11** know the price of this? For one teaspoonful, which is sufficient, I ask five thousand dollars. Never less. Not a penny less."
35 "I hope all your mixtures are not as expensive," said Alan **12** apprehensively.

"Oh dear, no," said the old man. "It would be no good **13** charging that sort of price for a love potion, for example. Young people who need a love potion very rarely have five thousand
40 dollars. Otherwise they would not need a love potion."

"I am glad to hear that," said Alan. **14**

"I look at it like this," said the old man. "Please a customer **15** with one article, and he will come back when he needs another even if it is more costly. He will save up for it, if necessary."
45 "So," said Alan, "you really do sell love potions?" **16**

"If I did not sell love potions," said the old man, reaching **17** for another bottle, "I should not have mentioned the other matter to you. It is only when one is able to help that one can afford to be so confidential."
50 "And these potions," said Alan. "They are not just—just— **18** er—"

"Oh, no," said the old man. "Their effects are permanent, **19** and extend beyond the mere casual impulse. But they include it. Oh, yes they include it. Bountifully, insistently. Everlastingly."
55 "Dear me!" said Alan, attempting a look of scientific **20** detachment. "How very interesting!"

"But consider the spiritual side," said the old man. **21**

"I do, indeed," said Alan. **22**

"For indifference," said the old man, "they substitute **23**
60 devotion. For scorn, adoration. Give one tiny measure of this to the young lady—its flavour is imperceptible in orange juice, soup, or cocktails—and however happy and giddy she is, she will change altogether. She will want nothing but solitude and you."
65 "I can hardly believe it," said Alan. "She is so fond of **24** parties."

"She will not like them any more," said the old man. "She **25** will be afraid of the pretty girls you may meet."

"She will actually be jealous?" cried Alan in a rapture. **26**
70 "Of me?"

"Yes, she will want to be everything to you." **27**

"She is, already. Only she doesn't care about it." **28**

"She will, when she has taken this. She will care intensely. **29** You will be her only interest in life."
75 "Wonderful!" cried Alan. **30**

"She will want to know all you do," said the old man. "All **31** that has happened to you during the day. Every word of it. She will want to know what you are thinking about, why you smile suddenly, why you are looking sad."
80 "That is love!" cried Alan. **32**

>>

"Yes," said the old man. "How carefully she will look [33] after you! She will never allow you to be tired, to neglect your food. If you are an hour late, she will be terrified. She will think you are killed, or that some **siren** has

85 caught you."

"I can hardly imagine Diana like that!" cried Alan, [34] overwhelmed with joy.

"You will not have to use your imagination," said the old [35] man. "And, by the way, since there are always sirens, if by any

90 chance you should, later on, slip a little, you need not worry. She will forgive you, in the end. She will be terribly hurt, of course, but she will forgive you—in the end."

"That will not happen," said Alan fervently. [36]

"Of course not," said the old man. "But, if it did, you [37]

95 need not worry. She would never divorce you. Oh, no! And, of course, she will never give you reasons to not trust her."

"And how much," said Alan, "is this wonderful mixture?" [38]

"It is not as **dear**," said the old man, "as the glove [39] cleaner, or life cleaner, as I sometimes call it. No. That is five

100 thousand dollars, never a penny less. One has to be older than you are, to indulge in that sort of thing. One has to save up for it."

"But the love potion?" said Alan. [40]

"Oh, that," said the old man, opening the drawer in the [41]

105 kitchen table, and taking out a tiny, rather dirty-looking phial. "That is just a dollar."

"I can't tell you how grateful I am," said Alan, watching [42] him fill it.

"I like to help," said the old man. "Then customers come [43]

110 back, later in life, when they are better off, and want more expensive things. Here you are. You will find it very effective."

"Thank you again," said Alan. "Good-bye." [44]

"Au revoir," said the man. [45]

1043 words

Short Story Elements

Read the story carefully and complete the chart.

Elements	Your Description
1. The Plot	
2. The Setting	
3. The Characters	Alan:
	Diana:
	Old man:
4. The Theme	
5. Your Reaction	

Glossary

dim landing (exp.) → dark front step

siren (n.) → seductive woman

dear (adj.) → expensive

📖 How To

UNDERSTAND A SHORT STORY

All well-written short fiction follows a similar pattern and contains certain elements. Analyzing these elements is rewarding as it brings a better understanding of the story.

The plot → What happens in the story?

The setting → Where and when does the story takes place?

The characters → What are their personality traits, values, ambitions, hopes, and fears? Do they learn something or evolve throughout the story? Do you like them or can you relate to them?

The theme → What is the main meaning or message of the story?

Comprehension

1. What is the meaning of the title "The Chaser"?

_____

_____

2. Reread the introductory paragraph and underline all of the descriptive language. Describe the following:

a. What You See	b. What You Feel	c. What You Hear

3. According to the old man, how will the potion change Diana? What is Alan's reaction to this promise?

_____

_____

_____

4. Why is the love potion so inexpensive?

_____

_____

5. What is a "glove cleaner" or "life cleaner"? How much does it cost? Why is it so expensive?

_____

_____

_____

Focus on Language: Mixed Verb Tenses

Fill in the blank with the missing auxiliary. Check your answers in paragraph 31.

"She _____^{1} want to know all you do," said the old man. " All that _____^{2} happened to you during the day. Every word of it. She _____^{3} want to know what you _____^{4} thinking about, why you smile suddenly, why you _____^{5} looking sad."

Writing

▶ Refer to Writing Files 2, page 65, for information on essay writing, and Writing Files 3, page 109, for information on improving your essay.

Write a short essay explaining one of the many valuable life lessons about love and relationships explored in "The Chaser" or in the unit. In your introduction be sure to write a thesis statement that clearly states the life lesson you will be exploring in the essay. Here is a short list of some themes you could write about:

☐ the consequences of possessive love

☐ the mistakes people make in their relationships

☐ the fact that you cannot force someone to love you

☐ the cost of fake love

☐ the dangers of jealousy and devotion

☐ the desperation to find true love

Relationships

If love really makes the world go around, then you should learn these common idiomatic expressions about love, dating, and relationships.

Match each expression with its definition. Then interview a partner to find out more about his or her relationship history. Record your partner's answers in the chart below. When you ask your partner questions, use the present perfect form: "Have you ever . . . ?"

Have you ever . . .	Meaning	Partner's Answers
1. fallen in love?	h	
2. broken someone's heart?		
3. gone on a double date?		
4. gone on a blind date?		
5. broken up with someone?		
6. given someone a second chance?		
7. been engaged?		
8. gone Dutch?		
9. had a crush on someone?		
10. been head over heels in love with someone?		

Meaning

a. gone on a date with someone you have never met

b. gone on a date with your partner and another couple

c. been very much in love with someone

d. caused emotional pain

e. ended a relationship

f. saved a relationship by forgiving your partner

g. agreed to marry someone

h. felt love for someone

i. gone on a date where you and your partner paid your own expenses

j. had strong feelings for someone for a short time

Grammar Link

PRESENT PERFECT AND SIMPLE PAST

Use the present perfect to talk about activities or events that happened at an indefinite time in the past and that have present relevance.

***Have** you ever **gone** on a blind date?*

Use the simple past to give details of the story.

*Yes, I **went** on a blind date once last summer. It **was** awful. My date **arrived** late, **ordered** the most expensive meal, and **expected** me to pay for it all.*

> Refer to *REAL Grammar Book 2*, units 4 and 7.

Write a text or give an oral presentation on one of the following topics. Try to incorporate the elements seen in the unit from the Make the Connection box and use as many of the Top Words as you can, where appropriate.

Make the Connection

- ☐ Present perfect
- ☐ Simple past
- ☐ Descriptive adjectives
- ☐ Vocabulary and idioms from the unit
- ☐ Pronouncing stressed syllables
- ☐ Activating prior knowledge
- ☐ Understanding a short story
- ☐ Question formation
- ☐ Giving your opinion using *should*
- ☐ Essay writing

▶ **Refer to Writing Files 2, page 65, for information on essay writing.**

▶ **Refer to appendix 1, page 155 for information on oral presentations.**

Vocabulary from the unit and other theme-related vocabulary can be practised online.

1 THE SCIENCE OF ATTRACTION: Why do opposites attract? Explain the scientific and evolutionary reasons why we fall in love with someone.

2 VIRTUAL LOVE: Is it possible to fall in love with someone you meet through online technology? How have online dating and virtual reality changed the way we fall in love?

3 RELATIONSHIP PERSONALITY: Are you a builder, a negotiator, an explorer, or a director? Helen Fisher, an expert on love, has written a book about these love personalities. Which relationship personalities fit together best?

4 ARRANGED MARRIAGES: With a 50% divorce rate in North America, are arranged marriages really such a bad idea? What is the success rate of arranged marriages? Present the negative and positive aspects of arranged marriages.

5 RELATIONSHIP MISTAKES: Why do relationships fail? What are some common mistakes couples make in their relationship? What relationships succeed?

6 OTHER: _____ Write about another topic of your choice linked to what you learned in this unit. Make sure to have your topic approved by your teacher.

Top Words

Put a check mark next to the words you know and refer to the page numbers to learn the ones you don't know. Add to the list other words that you want to remember from the unit.

ADJECTIVES	NOUNS	VERBS	EXPRESSIONS
☐ **annoying** (81)	☐ **attraction** (75)	☐ **to cheat** (75)	☐ **a blind date** (84)
☐ **dedicated** (81)	☐ **health** (75)	☐ **to commit** (75)	☐ **to hit it off** (78)
☐ **dependable** (81)	☐ **looks** (75)	☐ **to cuddle** (75)	☐ **to take my mind off** (78)
☐ **playful** (81)	☐ **wedding** (78)	☐ **to date** (84)	
☐ **restless** (81)			
☐ **sensuous** (81)			
☐ **shallow** (78)		**OTHER:**	
☐ **stubborn** (81)		_____	
☐ **successful** (81)		_____	

What's Your Impression?

The effects of first impressions and stereotypes

> How long does it take to form
> a first impression?

> Why are we so quick to judge?

> What impact do stereotypes
> and bias have on us?

In this unit, you will learn how
assumptions, first impressions,
and stereotypes affect your
judgment.

JUMPING TO CONCLUSIONS

Do You Judge a Book by Its Cover?

glance (n.) → rapid look

With just a quick **glance**, you can form an opinion about someone based on appearance, body language, and mannerisms. What assumptions do you make about people in this short time? How important are these impressions?

Grammar Link

COMPARATIVES AND SUPERLATIVES

Use a comparative adjective to compare two people, things, or groups.
*My sister is **older** and **funnier** than I am.*

Use a superlative adjective to compare more than two people, things, or groups.
*I am **the most intelligent** person in my family!*

To form them:
Most adjectives with one syllable: Add -er or -est
*fast, fast**er**, fast**est***

Most adjectives with two syllables: Use *more* or *the most*
*intelligent, **more** intelligent, **the most** intelligent*

Most adjectives with two syllables ending in -y:
Replace -y with -ier or -iest
*funny, funn**ier**, funn**iest***

Adverbs can also be used in the comparative and superlative form.
*You must work **more diligently** to pass the test.*
*Who works **the most diligently** on your team?*

▶ Refer to *REAL Grammar Book 2,* unit 6.

Look at the following pictures. Complete the questions with superlatives formed from the adjectives in the first column. Then take turns asking and answering the questions with your partner. Explain the reasons for your assumptions.

Samuel   Josh   Melanie   Karen   Zania   Ian

Adjective	Who is the . . . ?	Answer and Reason
1. athletic	most athletic	
2. attractive		
3. caring		
4. friendly		
5. funny		
6. intelligent		
7. rich		
8. shy		
9. social		
10. successful		

Discussion

1. How long did it take you to form a first impression about these people?

2. What attributes helped you most in forming this first impression? Explain.
   a. body language   **b.** clothing   **c.** facial expression   **d.** other

3. Did you and your partner make similar assumptions? Why or why not?

4. What role do the media play in the assumptions we make?

 READING   **FOR STRATEGY · TIMED READING**

It takes only a few seconds for you to form an opinion about someone you meet for the first time. How accurate are these first impressions?

Listen to "As If!" online to learn more about the importance of first impressions and bias.

Vocabulary

Match each word or expression with its correct definition before you read. The line number is in parentheses.

1.	an encounter (n., 1)	**a.**	a preference that prevents objective judgment
2.	to overwhelm (v., 2)	**b.**	correctly representing the truth
3.	the truth (n., 8)	**c.**	someone you know but who is not a close friend
4.	an acquaintance (n., 37)	**d.**	a verified or proven fact
5.	distrust (n., 51)	**e.**	to overpower
6.	a gut reaction (n., 55)	**f.**	after a quick, initial look
7.	a belief (n., 62)	**g.**	an immediate feeling or opinion
8.	a bias (n., 77)	**h.**	a feeling of suspicion or doubt
9.	at first glance (exp., 116)	**i.**	an opinion that you think is true
10.	accurate (adj., 104)	**j.**	an unplanned or brief meeting

Define each phrasal verb in the following sentences, using the definitions in the word box. The line number from the article is in parentheses.

> are important factors in   emit   leave   notice

1. We **walk away from** (_____) initial encounters with a first impression. (4)

2. New experiences **give off** (_____) signals. (23)

3. We can **pick up** (_____) a smile from 30 metres away. (29)

4. Implicit attitudes **enter into** (_____) our calculations. (60)

Grammar Link

PHRASAL VERBS

Phrasal verbs are very common in English. They consist of a verb followed by a preposition or an adverb, or both. The preposition or adverb adds a new meaning to the verb.

Turn on the music → make the music play

Turn off the music → make the music stop

Turn up the music → increase the volume

Turn down the music → decrease the volume

Look up the meaning of a phrasal verb in a general English dictionary or a dictionary of phrasal verbs.

▶ Refer to *REAL Grammar Book 2,* appendix 6.

Sometimes, the slower you read, the more difficult it is to remember the content. In fact, reading faster could help you understand better. Reading quickly is a skill that you can learn by timing yourself when you read. The more you practise, the faster you will read.

To become a fast reader, you should:

- Guess the meaning of unknown vocabulary.
- Predict what will happen next.
- Concentrate completely on what you are reading.
- Relax and enjoy the reading experience.

snap (adj.) → quick

clues (n.) → information that helps you to find an answer

Polaroid picture (n.) → snapshot

thin slices (n.) → very small amounts

applicants (n.) → candidates

likeability (n.) → appeal

semblance (n.) → outward appearance

Timed Reading

Read the article below quickly without stopping. Record your time. Answer the following questions.

1. How long did it take you to read the article? _____

2. How much of the article did you understand in this fast reading?

☐ All   ☐ Most   ☐ Some   ☐ None

3. What reading strategies did you use in this timed reading that allowed you to read faster and to understand at the same time?

_____

_____

4. Circle the main idea of this article that completes the sentence "The article by Carlin Flora called 'The Once Over' is about . . ."

a. Polaroid pictures

b. the Implicit Association Test

c. the importance of first impressions

d. how to do well in a job interview

The Once-Over

By Carlin Flora
Psychology Today

Initial encounters are emotionally concentrated events that can overwhelm us—even convince us that the room is spinning. We walk away from them with a first
5 impression that is like a **Polaroid picture**—a head-to-toe image that develops instantly and never entirely fades. Often, that snapshot captures important elements of the truth.

Consider one study in which untrained
10 subjects were shown videotaped segments, 20 to 32 seconds in length, of job **applicants** welcoming interviewers. The subjects then rated the applicants on attributes such as self-assurance and **likeability**. Surprisingly, their
15 evaluations were very close to those of trained interviewers who spent at least 20 minutes with each applicant. What **semblance** of

a person—one with a distinct appearance, history, and complex personality—could be
20 captured in such a short time?

The answer lies in part in how the brain takes first-impression Polaroids, creating an image of all the signals given off by a new experience. Psychologists agree that **snap**
25 judgments are a phenomenon in which **clues** (your voice, clothes, hairstyle, handshake, etc.) hit us all at once and form an impression. We search for one particular sign on a new face: a smile. "We can pick up a smile from
30 30 metres away," says Paul Ekman, professor of psychology at the University of California Medical School in San Francisco, and a pioneer of research on facial expressions. "A smile lets us know that we're likely to get a positive
35 greeting, and it's hard not to reciprocate."

Just three seconds are sufficient to make a conclusion about new acquaintances. Nalini Ambady, professor of psychology at Tufts University in Medford, Massachusetts,
40 studies first impressions taken from brief exposure to another person's behaviour, what she calls "**thin slices**" of experience. She says humans have developed the ability to quickly decide whether a new person
45 will hurt or enrich us—judgments that had lifesaving results in an earlier era.

She believes that thin slices are generated in the most primitive area of the brain, where feelings are also processed,

>>

which accounts for the emotional impact of
some first encounters. Immediate distrust
of a certain car salesperson or affinity for
a potential roommate originates in the
deepest regions of the mind.

First impressions are not merely gut
reactions. We are also taught how to judge
others, based on social stereotypes. Brian
Nosek, professor of psychology at the
University of Virginia, studies the implicit
attitudes that enter into our calculations.
Nosek and his colleagues administer a
quick online test that reveals the beliefs
people either can't or won't report.

Called the Implicit Association Test, it
asks participants to match concepts, such
as "young" with "good," or "elderly" with
"good." If, in some part of the test taker's
mind, "old" is more closely related to "bad"
than to "good," he or she will respond
more quickly to the first matching of
words than to the second. In versions of
these tests, small differences in response
times are used to determine if someone is
biased toward the young over the elderly,
or African-Americans over Caucasians,
for example. "When I took the test,"
says Nosek, "I showed a bias toward
white people. I was **shocked**. We call it
unconsciousness-raising."

As subtle as implicit attitudes
are, they can cause serious real-world
damage. If an angry person sees someone
of a different race or religion, he or she is
likely to perceive that person negatively,
according to research. Anger **incites**
instinctive prejudiced responses toward
"outsiders."

Certain physical features consistently
prompt our brains to create false first-
impression Polaroids. People who have a
"baby face," characterized by a round shape,
large eyes, and a small nose and chin, give
the impression of **trustworthiness** and
naïveté—on average, a false assumption.
A pretty face also leads us to false
assumptions. Our tendency is to perceive
beautiful people as healthier and better
than others.

Not every observer is equally likely to
make incorrect conclusions about a man
or a woman with beautiful symmetrical
features. People who spend time
cultivating relationships are more likely to
make accurate snap judgments. "A good
judge of personality isn't just someone
who is smarter. It's someone who spends
time with people," says David Funder, a
professor of psychology at the University of
California at Riverside, who believes in the
overall accuracy of snap judgments. Funder
has found that two observers often reach
a consensus about a third person, and the
assessments are correct in that they match
the third person's assessment of himself.

On the other side of the equation,
some people are simpler to capture at first
glance than others. "The people who are the
easiest to judge are the healthiest mentally,"
says Randy Colvin, associate professor of
psychology at Northeastern University in
Boston. "With mentally healthy individuals,"
Colvin theorizes, "exterior behaviour
mimics their internal views of themselves.
What you see is what you get."

804 words

trustworthiness (n.) → the quality of being honest, reliable, and dependable

shocked (adj.) → very surprised

incites (v.) → causes

Comprehension

Read the article again. Circle T or F to indicate if each statement is true or false. If it is false, write the correct statement on the line provided.

1. A first impression is like an old photograph: faded, unclear.   T   F

_____

2. People who saw only short videos of job candidates came to   T   F
basically the same conclusion about the candidates as experienced
interviewers who spent 20 minutes with them.

_____

3. We make snap judgments based only on physical appearance.   **T**   **F**

_____

4. It only takes a few seconds to make a judgment about a new person.   **T**   **F**

_____

5. The ability to make quick judgments about people helped our ancestors stay safe.   **T**   **F**

_____

6. Social stereotypes teach us how to judge people and they influence our first impression.   **T**   **F**

_____

7. The Implicit Association Test measures our conscious bias.   **T**   **F**

_____

8. A beautiful face can lead us to false assumptions and incorrect first impressions.   **T**   **F**

_____

▶ Refer to the Grammar Link on page 92 for more information on comparatives and superlatives.

Focus on Language: Comparatives and Superlatives

When you make assumptions about people, you usually compare them with something or someone you know, or with a group. You use the comparative and superlative forms to do this.

Scan the text for comparative and superlative adjectives and adverbs, and highlight them. Then write them in the correct column below.

Comparative	Superlative

Discussion and Writing

"As subtle as implicit attitudes are, they can cause serious real-world damage."

1. What does the author mean in this quote from the article?

2. What are some examples of these implicit attitudes?

3. What damage can these implicit attitudes cause?

4. Where do these attitudes come from? How can we change them?

Idioms

First Impressions

Are you dressed for success? Some idiomatic expressions encourage us to make a good first impression. Others warn us about judging someone too quickly.

Draw a line to connect the beginning of each idiom to its ending.

1. To put your best foot   by its cover.

2. You can't judge a book   leap.

3. Beauty is only   forward.

4. To get off on the wrong   of an eye.

5. In the blink   foot.

6. Beauty is in the eye   a conclusion.

7. To jump to   skin deep.

8. To look before you   of the beholder.

Use the idioms in context. Complete the sentence with the most appropriate idiom above.

1. You want to make a good first impression on your first date, so you

   _____.

2. If you and your classmate had a fight on your first day of class, you could say you

   _____.

3. Your parents taught you not to make judgments based only on appearances.

   They often said, _____.

4. You should always think about the possible risks before you do something. In

   other words, you should _____.

5. If you made a decision about someone too quickly, you

   _____.

6. Something that happens extremely quickly happens

   _____.

7. What's more important to you, personality or good looks? Personality is more

   important because _____.

8. Personally, I can't understand why she finds him attractive, but they do say

   _____.

The /h/ sound

To pronounce the /h/ sound in English, blow air through the mouth and begin to pronounce the vowel sound that follows the h, as in the words *hear* and *happy*.

Sometimes, the h is silent, as in the words *hour* and *honour*.

If you do not pronounce the /h/ sound correctly, or if you pronounce it when you shouldn't, it can sometimes lead to confusion.
I really like your heart.
But what you meant to say was:
I really like your art.

Listen to the tongue twister and repeat what you hear.

If Harry Hunt hunts heavy hairy hares,
Where are the heavy hairy hares Harry Hunt hunts?
Hurry, Harry! Hurry, Harry! Hurry, Harry!

Write down each word you hear. Put a checkmark in the appropriate column to indicate the beginning sound of each word.

	/h/	Vowel		/h/	Vowel		/h/	Vowel
1.			7.			13.		
2.			8.			14.		
3.			9.			15.		
4.			10.			16.		
5.			11.			17.		
6.			12.			18.		

Listen carefully to these sentences. Underline the letter *h* when it is pronounced and circle it when it is silent. Then repeat the sentences after the speaker.

1. The heir to the fortune was assumed to be homeless yet honourable.

2. How can we help him not to make assumptions about hip hoppers?

3. The human library is a helpful place where we can confront our harmful biases honestly.

4. You have one hour to discuss your stereotype.

Create four sentences on a separate piece of paper using as many words as possible from the chart above.

Dictate your sentences to your partner and then listen to his or her sentences.
Write what you hear on a separate piece of paper. Compare your sentences with your partner's originals. Did your partner pronounce the /h/ sounds correctly?

💬 SPEAKING | In the Blink of an Eye

Whether you're meeting your classmates, starting a new job, or going on a date, there's always some tension when you meet someone for the first time.

Discuss first encounters in small groups. Try to use at least two idiomatic expressions from the Idioms section in your discussion.

- Describe a memorable first encounter you had with an important person in your life. Describe in detail where you met this person and the first impression you formed. Was this first impression correct?

- When people meet you for the first time, what impression do you think they generally form of you? Is this first impression usually accurate?

- Do you think people get a second chance to make a good first impression? Explain.

👁 WATCHING | Borrow a Stereotype

Are you aware of any stereotypes you hold of certain groups of people? If you could borrow a human book to help you challenge those stereotypes, would you? Watch this CBC television report about the launch of the first Living Library project in North America.

Vocabulary

Make sure you understand the definitions of the following words before you watch the documentary.

1. a library (n.) → a place where you can borrow books

2. to launch (v.) → to introduce

3. to borrow (v.) → to use something that belongs to someone else for a limited time

4. to stab (v.) → to pierce with a sharp object like a knife

5. to break down the stereotypes (v.) → to eliminate the stereotypes

6. to check out a book (v.) → to borrow a book from a library

Comprehension

Read the questions. Then watch the video and answer them.

1. Who is Ronni Abergel?

a. How old is he?	b. Where is he from?	c. What did he do?	d. Why is he in L.A.?

2. What is the Living Library?

a. How is it different from a library with books?	b. What is the goal of the Living Library?

3. The video mentions members of groups that are stereotyped. Name four of them.

a. _____   c. _____

b. _____   d. _____

4. What happened to the police officer when he was "borrowed" by three members of the extreme left movement?

_____

5. When Ronni was 14, he was intolerant of a group of people. Which one?

_____

6. Who is Leslie?

a. What type of "book" is she?	b. Who "borrowed" her?	c. What questions was she asked?

7. According to the homeless book, is homelessness a preference?

_____

_____

8. What happened to Ronni when he was 19 years old? What impact did this have on him?

_____

_____

9. What emotion do people feel after a Living Library meeting?

_____

10. Fill in the blanks with the words you hear.

Ronni says: "With the Living Library, I'm hoping to stimulate the creation of those

_____ ᵃ across the community so that . . . if we get in a _____ ᵇ,

instead of burning down each other's neighbourhoods, we're going to sit down and

_____ ᶜ about things."

Discussion

1. Is the Living Library a successful project? Explain by referring to what the participants said in the report.

2. If you could borrow a book from the Living Library, what type of book would you borrow? Why? What would you ask this book?

Writing

Write an essay on the role the media play in reinforcing and perpetuating stereotypes. Choose one of the following groups of people and focus your essay on the ways this group is stereotyped.

Read "Youth Stereotyping and Its Impact" online to learn more about the role media plays in reinforcing stereotypes about teenagers.

☐ Aboriginal people   ☐ Homosexuals

☐ Elderly people   ☐ Religious people

☐ Females   ☐ Teenagers

☐ Homeless people   ☐ Other visible minority _____

- Demonstrate how this group is portrayed in the media by giving specific examples from popular movies, TV shows, books, and the news.
- Explain the impact this portrayal or stereotype has on both the group and society in general.
- Suggest ways to change this kind of negative stereotyping. If you see a more fair portrayal of this group in the media, then discuss it in your essay as well.

Refer to Writing Files 2, page 65, for information on essay writing, and Writing Files 3, page 109, for information on improving your essay.

 READING   **FOR INTERACTION**

Studies show that even though some stereotypes are untrue, they can affect the way we perform. There are also reports that reveal that we unconsciously prefer attractiveness.

Discussion

1. Who usually does better at math and science: girls or boys? Who does better at languages? Who is better at using computers? Who are the better readers?

2. Do attractive people have an advantage in society? Why or why not?

3. Are tall men more successful in today's society? Why or why not?

Work in pairs. One student reads the study about women and math, and the other reads the study about beauty bias. Do the vocabulary activities for the study you chose. Then complete the chart on page 104.

Vocabulary

Read the first paragraph of the article "Women and Math." Find a synonym from the word list in the margin for each word in bold. Write the synonym on the line provided. Then read the rest of the article.

abilities   more poorly
connecting   subjected
influence

1. _____

2. _____

3. _____

4. _____

5. _____

reminding (n.) → causing to remember

threat (n.) → possible danger, menace

bogus (adj.) → fake

fate (n.) → destiny

Women and Math

CBC News

Women **exposed**[1] to bogus scientific theories **linking**[2] their gender to poor math **skills**[3] did **worse**[4] on arithmetic tests than others, according to a study that
5   suggests that even false stereotypes about genetic makeup can **sway**[5] performance.

The three-year study at the University of British Columbia involved 135 women taking challenging math tests similar to those used
10   for graduate school entrance exams. Before they were given the test, the women were required to read one of four essays—three of them about gender difference in math. One essay argued there was no difference,
15   a second argued the difference was genetic, and a third said the difference was the result of social construction and the way girls were taught in elementary school. The fourth essay covered the subject of women in art.
20   Research has shown that simply **reminding** a person that he or she falls into some stereotyped category can change the person's performance, in what is known as a stereotype **threat**. When the women were
25   told **bogus** scientific theories about being born bad at math, they did worse, says the study, which was published in the journal *Science*. The women who were told that prior experience determined their math ability got
30   twice as many answers right on the exam as women who were told their genetics were to blame, the researchers said.

"So, when they hear there's a gene for math, and they might not have it, they can
35   be affected," said Ilan Dar-Nimrod, a doctoral student in social psychology and the lead author of the study "Exposure to Scientific Theories Affects Women's Math Performance."

Dar-Nimrod said the latest study shows
40   genetics-based theories—even if they're bogus—can be powerful.

"And I think that's what the study shows," he told the CBC. "They are much more affected than if they hear that people from
45   their own neighbourhood, or people who went to their school, are not good in math."

Steven Heine, an associate professor of social psychology at UBC and co-author of the study, said the study should force
50   researchers and the media to be more cautious when talking about a "gene" for obesity or other diseases because most people incorrectly see genes as **fate**.

"People seem to interpret it as meaning
55   that if I have this gene I must become obese," he said.

"The relations between genes and behaviour are very complex and unfortunately people do view them in more deterministic
60   terms than they should."

407 words

Vocabulary

Read the first paragraph of the article "Beauty Bias." Find a synonym from the word list in the margin for each word in bold. Write the synonym on the line provided. Then read the rest of the article.

Beauty Bias

Science Daily

We might not be able to resist a **pretty**[1] face after all, according to a report from the University of Pennsylvania. Experiments in which **subjects**[2] were given a fraction of a second to judge "**attractiveness**[3]" offered further evidence that our preference for beauty might be **hard-wired**[4]. People who participated in the studies were also more likely to associate pretty faces with positive **traits**[5].

"We're able to judge attractiveness with surprising speed and on the basis of very little information," said Ingrid Olson, a professor in Penn's department of psychology and researcher at Penn's Centre for Cognitive Neuro-science. "It seems that pretty faces 'prime' our minds to make us more likely to associate the pretty face with a positive emotion."

Olson, along with co-author Christy Marshuetz of Yale University, recently published their findings in the journal *Emotion*, a publication of the American Psychological Association. The researchers **set out** to study cognitive processes behind a very real phenomenon: physically attractive people have advantages that unattractive people do not.

"Research has demonstrated **time and again** that there are tremendous social and economic benefits to being attractive," Olson said. "Attractive people are paid more, are judged more intelligent, and will receive more attention in most aspects of life."

"This favouritism, while poorly understood, seems to be innate and cross-cultural. Studies suggest that even infants prefer pretty faces," Olson said. In their report, the researchers describe three experiments to investigate the preference for attractiveness.

The first study tested the idea that beauty can be assessed rapidly by asking study participants to **rate** pictures of faces of non-famous males and females. The photos were taken from three different high-school yearbooks and the Internet, and appeared for .013 seconds on a computer screen.

Although participants reported that they could not see the faces and that they were guessing on each trial, they were able to rate the attractiveness of those faces accurately.

"There are no definite rules to what kind of face can be called beautiful, but we chose faces of either extreme ugliness or prettiness," Olson said. "Seen rapidly, viewers were able to make an unconscious, but accurate, assessment of physical beauty."

In their second and third experiments, the researchers explored the notion of "priming"—whether or not seeing a pretty face makes a viewer more likely to associate that face with positive attributes. The second experiment involved rapidly showing a face on the screen, followed shortly by a word in white text on a black screen. Participants were instructed to ignore the face and were timed on how quickly they could classify the word as either good or bad. Almost uniformly, response times to good words, such as "laughter" or "happiness," were faster after viewing an attractive face.

"In a way, pretty faces are **rewarding**; they make us more likely to think good thoughts," said Olson. "There are some underlying processes going on in the brain that prejudice us to respond to attractive people better even if we are not **aware** of it."

They repeated the priming test in a third experiment, this time using images of houses, to see whether the beauty bias is a general phenomenon or one that is limited to socially important stimuli such as faces. Unlike faces, response times to good words were not faster after having viewed an attractive house.

"Faces hold a special power for us, perhaps more so than art or objects," Olson said. "The beauty bias has a real influence upon us, something we should be conscious of when dealing with others."

585 words

set out (v.) → planned

rewarding (adj.) → satisfying

time and again (exp.) → many times

aware (adj.) → conscious

rate (v.) → calculate the value of

1. _____
2. _____
3. _____
4. _____
5. _____

Comprehension

Fill in the chart with the information that corresponds to the study you chose. Ask your partner for the missing information from the study he or she read about, and complete the chart.

	Women and Math	Beauty Bias
1. What is the stereotype or bias?		
2. What is the theory?		
3. Explain the experiments.		
4. Explain the results of the experiments.		
5. What are the conclusions of the research study?		

LISTENING The Gender Trap

We have come to believe that men and women, and boys and girls, all have different brains. According to some neuroscientists and psychologists, however, the consequence of this belief is unhealthy gender stereotyping. An episode of *Ideas*, a CBC radio documentary series, explores the debate.

Discussion

1. What are the stereotypical characteristics of boys and girls? Fill in the chart below.

Boys	Girls

2. How do boys play? How do girls play? Did boys and girls learn to play this way or were they born with these differences?

3. Is it possible to raise a gender-neutral child? Explain why or why not.

Comprehension

Read the questions. Then listen to the radio documentary and answer them.

The Gender Debate: Born to Be Different

Some scientists believe that boys and girls are born to be different.

1. Fill in the blanks with the words you hear that describe these differences.

    a. They have different _____.

    b. They _____ differently.

    c. They _____ differently.

    d. Their sex makes them better suited to be a _____ or an _____.

    e. They are hard-wired to be better at _____ or to be more _____.

    f. Boys relate more to _____, girls connect more with _____.

    g. Gender is a powerful predictor of _____, style, _____, and achievement.

    h. This idea of an essential difference between boys and girls is fuelling movements for _____ in schools.

FYI

Experiences reorganize neural pathways in the brain. Long-lasting functional changes in the brain occur when we learn new things or memorize new information. These changes in neural connections are what we call *neuroplasticity*.

Stereotyped to Be Different

Other thinkers in the field believe that this "biological determinism" is based on gender stereotyping.

2. According to this side of the debate, what factors influence children's development?

   Neuroplasticity and _____ influence children's development.

3. According to Cordelia Fine, author of *Delusions of Gender*, which of these statements are correct? Circle all the correct answers.

   a. Sex difference in the brain is innate and unchangeable.
   b. The brain develops through interaction with experience and the environment.
   c. Differences in the brain do not mean there is a genetic cause.

Gender Neutral

4. Which of these statements describe Kathy Witterick and David Stocker's beliefs about gender stereotyping and gender in childhood? Circle all the correct answers.

   a. Gender stereotyping limits childhood.
   b. They believe there is fluidity to gender.
   c. They do not allow their boys to wear braids and dresses.
   d. They told everyone the gender of their third baby.

5. How are the boys dressed?

   _____

   _____

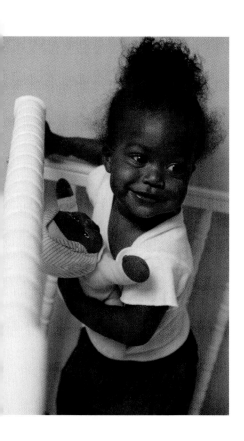

6. How many people know if Storm is a boy or a girl?

   _____

7. Why did the parents decide not to reveal his or her identity?

   _____

   _____

Gender-stereotyped Toys

8. Name some of the gender-stereotyped toys that are mentioned.

   _____

9. Are we more or less stereotyped now than in the past?   ☐ More   ☐ Less

10. Describe the difference between the Hot Wheels track made for boys and the one made for girls.

    _____

11. How were girls depicted on toys marketed to boys?

    _____

 **SPEAKING** # The Gender Debate

After listening to the radio documentary about the gender trap, it is time to debate!

Form teams according to your teacher's instructions. Choose a captain and a secretary. Brainstorm arguments to support your side of the debate. Record your ideas below.

Born to Be Different	Socialized to Be Different
Boys and girls are genetically hard-wired to be different.	Boys and girls are different because of the stereotypes society has created for them.

Conduct the debate. Use the expressions in the How To to help you express your ideas and opinions.

1. Each team gives a summary of the situation and the main arguments that support the position.

2. Each team will have a chance to disagree with the other team's arguments.

3. Your teacher will decide which team developed and presented the best arguments and used the most effective debating language.

💬 How To

USE DEBATING LANGUAGE

Study this debating language before you begin your debate. Try to use as many of these expressions as you can while debating your point of view with your classmates.

Stating an Opinion	Asking for an Opinion	Expressing Agreement	Expressing Disagreement	Interruptions
In my opinion . . .	What's your idea?	That's so true.	I don't think so.	Can I add something here?
According to Lisa, . . .	How do you feel about that?	That's exactly how I feel.	(strong) I totally disagree.	If I might add something, . . .
As far as I'm concerned, . . .	What do you think?	Absolutely.	Not necessarily.	Sorry to interrupt, but . . .
If you ask me, . . .	Do you have anything to say about this?	I agree with James.	That's not always true.	

Topic Files

Write a text or give an oral presentation on one of the following topics. Try to incorporate the elements seen in the unit from the Make the Connection box and use as many of the Top Words as you can, where appropriate.

1 FIRST IMPRESSIONS: How long does it take to form a first impression? Are these impressions usually correct? Research this topic to discover why we are hard-wired to make judgments about people.

2 UNCONSCIOUS BIAS: Do you have an unconscious bias? Explain the impact these unconscious biases have on society.

3 THE HUMAN LIBRARY: If you could go to a human library and "borrow a stereotype," what book would you take out? Explain why. What would you ask your book and what would you hope to learn? Is the human library a good way to break down barriers and rid society of stereotypes?

4 BEAUTY BIAS: What is the beauty bias and what impact does it have on society? Is this bias fair and what can we do to change it?

5 GENDER DIFFERENCES: Are boys and girls born different or are they socialized to be different? Research this topic to find out what experts say.

6 OTHER: _____ Write about another topic of your choice linked to what you learned in this unit. Make sure to have it approved by your teacher.

Make the Connection

- ☐ Comparatives and superlatives
- ☐ Phrasal verbs
- ☐ Vocabulary and idioms related to stereotypes and first impressions
- ☐ Pronouncing the /h/ sound
- ☐ Doing timed readings
- ☐ Using debating language
- ☐ Academic essay

▶ Refer to Writing Files 2, page 65, and Writing Files 3, page 109, for more information on writing and improving essays.

▶ Refer to appendix 1, page 155, for more information on oral presentations.

Vocabulary from the unit and other theme-related vocabulary can be practised online.

Top Words

Put a check mark next to the words you know and refer to the page numbers to learn the ones you don't know. Add to the list other words that you want to remember from the unit.

ADJECTIVES	EXPRESSIONS	NOUNS	VERBS
☐ **accurate** (93)	☐ **to break down** (99)	☐ **an acquaintance** (93)	☐ **to borrow** (99)
☐ **caring** (92)	☐ **to give off** (93)	☐ **a belief** (93)	☐ **to launch** (99)
☐ **exposed** (102)	☐ **to walk away from** (93)	☐ **a bias** (93)	☐ **to overwhelm** (93)
☐ **hard-wired** (103)		☐ **distrust** (93)	☐ **to sway** (102)
☐ **pretty** (103)		☐ **an encounter** (93)	
☐ **worse** (102)		☐ **a skill** (102)	
		☐ **a trait** (103)	

OTHER:

_____   _____

_____   _____

_____   _____

Improving Your Essay

The Introduction

First impressions are extremely important. This is why you need to pay special attention to the introduction of your essay. A strong introduction engages the readers' interest and encourages them to read the essay.

Refer to Writing Files 2, page 65, for more information on thesis statements.

The introductory paragraph contains **two** parts:

1. An **attention-getter** ► an opening sentence that grabs the readers' attention

2. The **thesis statement** ► a sentence that indicates the central idea of the essay and the main ideas that will be developed (This statement is usually placed at the end of the introduction.)

There are several kinds of **attention-getters** to choose from:

- A quotation or paraphrase ► *According to Statistics Canada, the youth crime rate has been steadily declining since 2007.*

- An interesting fact, statistic, or statement ► *It takes only three seconds to form a first impression, so be sure to dress for success.*

- A question ► *Did you know that society has a preference for a pretty face?*

- A challenge to a common opinion ► *Buying organic products does not help support small eco-farms and is not better for the environment.*

- An anecdote or story related to the topic ► *I can remember the first time I saw the commercial for the yellow Barbie dollhouse camper. I was six years old and I had to have it.*

Practice 1

Read the introduction below and do the following:

1. Underline the attention-getter.

2. Highlight the thesis statement.

3. Identify the attention-getting strategy used.

> Facebook is a social disaster! In the past, people connected with each other via the telephone or at school. Face-to-face communication was valued. Today, people hide behind their devices and connect with hundreds of friends virtually, but are they really communicating? Facebook is devoid of any real personal connectedness and doesn't allow for meaningful communication.

Attention-getting strategy: _____

Write It!

Choose one of the following topics and write two different introductions on a separate piece of paper. Use a different attention-getting strategy and thesis statement for each introduction. Put a star beside the introduction you prefer.

> the beauty bias
> first impressions
> marketing to millennials
> online marketing
> stereotyping
> other: _____

Transition Words

Transition words help to connect ideas. They create a clear and cohesive text. They are like the turn signals on a car—they let people know where you are going.

Here are some transition words and expressions that will make your writing more cohesive and easier to read.

Practice 2

Put a check mark next to the transition words and expressions that you know and already use in your writing. Look up any unfamiliar words or expressions in a dictionary. Write the definitions or translations in the spaces provided.

Chronology	☐ first	☐ next	☐ in the first place	☐ then
	☐ second	☐ meanwhile	☐ third	☐ finally
Addition	☐ also	☐ moreover	☐ furthermore	
	☐ in addition	☐ as well	☐ including	
Example	☐ for example	☐ to illustrate	☐ for instance	☐ in fact
Contrast	☐ although	☐ on the other hand	☐ however	☐ nevertheless
Result	☐ therefore	☐ thus	☐ consequently	☐ so
Emphasis	☐ clearly	☐ certainly	☐ in fact	☐ undoubtedly
Conclusion	☐ to conclude	☐ in short	☐ to sum up	☐ in conclusion

Write It!

Write one or two supporting paragraphs on a separate piece of paper for the introduction you wrote in the first Write It! exercise. Use and underline three transition words or expressions in your paragraphs. Highlight your topic sentences.

Refer to Writing Files 2, page 65, for more information on thesis statements.

The Conclusion

The concluding or last paragraph of the essay is your opportunity to make an impression on your reader. It represents your last chance to say something important. The conclusion has **two** main functions:

1. It **summarizes** or **reinforces** the main points of the essay.

2. It brings your essay to an interesting close with a **memorable statement**.

Do not contradict your main point or introduce a new idea in your conclusion. Do not apologize for your point of view.

There are several kinds of **memorable statements** to choose from:

- A thought-provoking quotation or question ▶ *As Malcolm Gladwell explains in Blink: The Power of Thinking Without Thinking, "Truly successful decision-making relies on a balance between deliberate and instinctive thinking."*
- A solution to a problem discussed in the essay ▶ *Next time you put the key in the ignition to drive to school, consider other stress-free and environmentally friendly options such as biking, walking, or taking public transport.*
- A suggestion for change ▶ *We should put aside our electronic gadgets to make time for meaningful face-to-face communication.*

Practice 3

Read the conclusion to the essay about youth stereotypes and the media below and do the following:

1. Highlight the concluding transition word.

2. Circle the summary of the main points.

3. Underline the memorable statement. What kind of statement is used? _____

> In conclusion, the media are powerful in creating and reinforcing stereotypes. The continuous negative portrayal of teenagers in the news and movies adversely affects the way society views young people and also changes society's expectations of them. People begin to believe that most teens, rather than just a few individuals, are dangerous and belong to gangs. To change this negative stereotype, the media need to offer a more balanced portrayal of youth in society.

Write It!

Write a conclusion on a separate piece of paper for one of your introductions from the first Write It! exercise. Be sure to use a transition word to indicate to the reader that you are concluding your essay.

Revising for Unity and Cohesion

Once you have written the first draft of your essay, you need to revise it to ensure that it is unified and cohesive. Reread it to make sure that all of the ideas are clear, connected, and well organized, and express what you really want to say.

Unity ensures that all the ideas are related.

- An essay is unified when all the ideas relate to the central idea or thesis statement.
- A paragraph is unified when every sentence develops the point made in the topic sentence. The paragraph must have a single focus and contain no irrelevant facts.

Cohesion is the logical, smooth natural flow from one idea to another in your essay. You can use helpful words and expressions to guide the reader through your text.

- **Transition words** help to connect sentences and paragraphs. They create a clear and cohesive text. Choose your transition words from the chart on page 110.

- **Coordinators,** such as *and, but, or, yet,* and *so,* help connect ideas within a sentence.

  *Today, people hide behind their devices **and** connect with hundreds of friends virtually, **but** are they really communicating?*

- **Subordinators,** such as *although, after, unless, until,* and *because,* join a subordinate idea to a main idea in a sentence.

  *Be sure to dress for success **because** it takes only three seconds to form a first impression.*

Ask yourself these questions to ensure the unity and cohesion of your essay:

1. Does every detail support the main idea?

2. Have I eliminated all ideas, sentences, or paragraphs that are not related to my thesis statement?

3. Is the organization of my ideas clear and logical?

4. Is the relationship between my ideas clear?

5. Do I use transition words and expressions to guide the reader?

Revise and Edit It!

Revise the following paragraph, which is missing a clear topic sentence and lacks unity and cohesion. Rewrite the paragraph on a separate piece of paper and do the following:

1. Create an effective topic sentence about youth and the media.

2. Eliminate any unrelated, unclear, or illogical ideas.

3. Reorganize the information so the relationship between the ideas is clear.

4. Incorporate and highlight transition words to show the relationship between one idea and the next.

> In a way, this impression is the media's fault. In general, the image that we have about something comes from something we have already seen or heard. The media does not give a fair picture of young people. Popular movies often portray teenagers as being in gangs, and being violent. These action movies are a lot of fun to watch. We should not show these inaccurate and harmful stereotypes about visible minorities. Kids are very influenced by what they see. They are stereotyped as drug addicts and aggressive people but it is only a part of them who are like that. According to Statistics Canada both youth homicide and youth charged with property offences have steadily decreased over the years. Negative stereotypes not only affect how adults see teenagers, they influence how teenagers see themselves.

Write It!

Use the checklists at the back of the book and all the information you learned in Writing Files 3 to revise, edit, and improve your own essay.

HAPPINESS

What Is the Price of Happiness?

The relationship between your life, money, and happiness

> What are more valuable to you: possessions or experiences?

> How important is being passionate about your work?

> Can people laugh their way to happiness?

In this unit, you will learn about the latest research on happiness theories.

LOOK ON THE BRIGHT SIDE

Are You a Spender or a Saver?

Does a healthy bank account put a smile on your face, or do you prefer to share the wealth?

Circle the image that most closely represents your relationship to money. Then write a sentence below, describing your relationship to money.

_____

_____

Answer the following questions by circling your response. Then survey three classmates about their relationship to money and record their answers in the columns.

	Student 1	Student 2	Student 3
1. What do you usually do with the money you earn? **a.** save it **b.** spend it			
2. For the most part, where does your money go? **a.** to pay bills and rent **d.** to save for university **b.** to buy clothes, gadgets, etc. **e.** to go out to movies, restaurants, etc. **c.** to pay for my car			
3. How often do you donate money to a charity or non-profit organization? **a.** regularly **b.** sometimes **c.** never			
4. If you see a homeless person on the street, do you give something? **a.** yes, always **b.** sometimes **c.** no, never			
5. What brings you happiness? **a.** spending money **d.** exercising **b.** spending time with friends and family **e.** other: _____ **c.** going on vacation			

Calculate the statistical data on your classmates' relationship to money. Work with a partner. The two of you should have answers from six classmates, plus your own, for a total of eight answers. If you both interviewed the same people, only count their answers once.

1. _____ % of students save their money.

2. _____ % of students use their money to pay for a car.

3. _____ % of students regularly donate money to charity.

4. _____ % of students regularly give money to the homeless.

5. _____ % of students believe money makes them happy.

 # Can Money Buy Happiness?

How much money does it take to be happy? In this debate activity, you and your classmates will explore the connection between money and happiness.

Form groups according to your teacher's instructions. You will be in a team that will try to prove that money can or can't buy happiness. Use the following chart to brainstorm arguments with your teammates.

Money *Can* Buy Happiness	Money *Can't* Buy Happiness

Grammar Link

MODALS

Modals are often used in debates because they help us express opinions, and agree and disagree in a polite way.

A modal is an auxiliary verb. When a modal is combined with a main verb, it expresses the following:

Ability
I **can** see your point, but . . .

Polite Requests
May I please add something?

Advice
We **should** focus on the topic.

Conditional
We **would** be happier if . . .

Possibility
It **could** be true that money buys happiness, but . . .
Money may make people happier, but . . .

Obligation
You **mustn't** believe everything you hear.

Modals come before the base form of the main verb.
She **should** earn more money.
(~~should to earn~~)

Modals do not take an -s in the third-person singular.
He **would** like to win the lottery.
(~~woulds like~~)

Conduct the debate, following the steps below. Use the modal expressions from the Grammar Link to help you express yourself politely.

1. Each team gives a summary of the situation and the main arguments that support their position.
2. Each team has a chance to disagree with the other team's arguments.
3. Your teacher will decide which team has developed and presented the best arguments, and used the most effective debating language.

Refer to *REAL Grammar Book 2,* unit 8.

Pronunciation

Can versus Can't

To hear the difference between **can** and **can't**, you have to listen to where the speaker puts the stress.

Can is normally reduced and the main verb is stressed.

*Money can **buy** happiness.* (pronounced "kin" buy)

Can't is always stressed.

*Money **can't** buy happiness.* (pronounced "kant" buy)

Listen to this tongue twister and repeat what you hear. Then say it as quickly as you can.

> *A canner exceedingly canny,*
> *one morning remarked to his granny,*
> *"A canner can can anything that he can,*
> *but a canner can't can a can, can he?"*

Listen to the sentences. Decide if they are affirmative or negative by circling *can* or *can't*. Repeat each sentence after the speaker.

1. can	can't		**5.** can	can't	
2. can	can't		**6.** can	can't	
3. can	can't		**7.** can	can't	can can't
4. can	can't		**8.** can	can't	

READING   FOR INTERACTION

Some experts say that money can't buy happiness, but others say we just need to spend our money on other people or on experiences to feel happiness. What do you say?

Discussion

1. How much money does a person need in order to be happy?

2. Can too much money lead to unhappiness?

3. What do you think makes you happier, money, experiences, or possessions?

Work in pairs. One student reads about a study of money and happiness, and the other student reads about a study of happiness and possessions. Do the vocabulary exercise for your chosen study as you read.

Vocabulary

Write a short definition or synonym on the line next to each word or expression in bold. Use context clues from the text to help you guess the meaning.

Money Can Buy You Happiness—If You Spend It on Others: Study

CBC News

People are happier when they **spend** money on others than when they spend it on themselves, a new study by researchers in Canada and the United States suggests.

"Our results suggest that how people spend their money is at least as important for happiness as how much they **earn**," co-author Lara Aknin told CBCNews.ca. "Therefore,
5 small alterations in your spending choices—even small amounts—can have a significant impact on your happiness level."

Aknin, along with lead author Elizabeth Dunn, an assistant professor of psychology, and Michael Norton, an assistant professor at the Harvard Business School, analyzed results from three reports on happiness and spending. In the first experiment, the researchers asked 632
10 people to report their annual income and the **breakdown** of their monthly spending and rank their general happiness.

"Regardless of how much **income** each person had . . . those who spent money on others reported greater happiness, while those who spent more on themselves did not," Dunn said.

15 The second analysis looked at the reactions of 16 employees when they received their bonuses, which ranged from $3 000 to $8 000. "Employees who devoted more of their bonus to prosocial spending on others experienced greater happiness after receiving the bonus, and the manner in which they spent that bonus was a more important predictor of their happiness than the size of the bonus itself," the report said.

20 For the final aspect of their study, the researchers gave 46 UBC-Vancouver campus students either $5 or $20 to spend in a day. They instructed half to spend the money on themselves and the rest to spend it on others. Like the results of the previous two studies, the researchers found that those who spent their money on others reported being happier.

25 "We found that spending more of one's income on others predicted greater happiness," Aknin said. "Finally, participants who were randomly assigned to spend money on others experienced greater happiness than those assigned to spend money on themselves."

Aknin said the research suggests "people can find more happiness by changing their
30 spending patterns—redirecting more to others in the form of **charity** and gift-giving." She said that, based on the study, she will try to spend more on others, adding, "I hope others do, too."

374 words

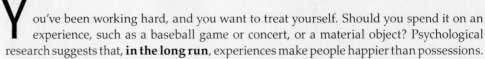

Study: Experiences Make Us Happier Than Possessions

By Elizabeth Landau
CNN

You've been working hard, and you want to treat yourself. Should you spend it on an experience, such as a baseball game or concert, or a material object? Psychological research suggests that, **in the long run**, experiences make people happier than possessions.

That's in part because the initial joy of acquiring a new object, such as a new car,
5 **fades** over time as people become accustomed to seeing it every day, experts say. Experiences, on the other hand, continue to provide happiness through memories long after the event occurs.

Ryan Howell, assistant professor of psychology at San Francisco State University, presented the findings of his study that looked at 154 university students with an average age of about 25. Participants answered questions about a **purchase**—either material or
10 experiential—they made in the last three months with the intention of making themselves happy.

While most people were generally happy with the purchase regardless of what it was, those who wrote about experiences tended to show a higher satisfaction at the time and after the experience had passed. The most striking difference was in how participants said others around them reacted to either the purchased object or experience. Experiences led to more
15 happiness in others than purchases did. A sense of **relatedness** to others—getting closer to friends and family—may be one of the reasons why experiences generate more happiness.

"When people spend money on life experiences, whether they also take someone with them or buy an extra ticket or whatever, most of our life experiences involve other individuals," Howell said. People were fulfilling their need for social **bonding** while having
20 these experiences, he claimed.

Another reason for increased happiness in experiences, the researchers found, was that people felt a greater sense of vitality or "being alive" during the experience and in reflection, Howell said. "As nice as your new computer is, it's not going to make you feel alive."

Most psychologists who study the phenomenon say people adapt to a new purchase in
25 six to eight weeks, up to a maximum of three months, Howell reported. That means the initial pleasure we get from a new possession generally fades in a matter of months.

Howell's study builds on earlier work by Thomas Gilovich, professor and chairman of the psychology department at Cornell University. Gilovich's paper "To do or to have: That is the question" found similar results about possessions bringing less happiness than experiences.
30 Experts also point out that people are less self-conscious when comparing experiences than they are about possessions. It will probably bother you more that your friend's home theatre is better than yours than if your friend saw more sights on her South Seas vacation, said Gilovich. Experiences form "powerful and important memories that I wouldn't trade for anything in the world," he stated.
35 According to Gilovich, it's not just individuals who should be thinking about investing in experiences when making purchasing choices. Policy makers should also keep this reasoning in mind for their communities. "If you create municipalities with more parks, bike trails, more hiking trails that make experiences easier, then I think you're going to have a happier population," he concluded.

520 words

Fill in the following chart with the information that corresponds to the study you read about.
Ask your partner for the missing information to complete the chart and to prepare for the discussion that follows.

	Money Can Buy You Happiness	Experiences Make Us Happier Than Possessions
Summarize the studies in your own words.		
Explain the results of the studies.		
Explain the conclusions.		

Discussion

1. What is the best, or most expensive, gift you've ever given someone? What did you give? Who did you give it to? What was the occasion? Explain the person's reaction to your gift. Describe your feelings after giving it. Do you agree that spending money on others brings happiness?

2. What is the best experience (trip, concert, activity) that you've ever spent your own money on? What did you do? Where did you go? Who did you go with? How did you feel at the time of the experience? How do you feel about the experience now that you are remembering it? Do you agree that spending money on experiences brings happiness?

📖 How To

Writing

Write an argumentative essay about the relationship between money and happiness. Refer to the How To in the margin for guidance.

Idioms

Money

Money talks! There are so many idiomatic expressions in English related to money, that one could say money really does talk!

Complete the following chart with the correct idiomatic expressions from the box then label the pictures with the correct number from the chart.

> Money burns a hole in your pocket.
> Money doesn't grow on trees.
> Money down the drain
> Money talks.
>
> On the money
> Time is money.
> To have money to burn

Image	Idiomatic Expression	Meaning
	Time is money.	Time is valuable and should not be wasted.
1.		To have so much money you can spend it any way you like
2.		Be careful about how much you spend, because the amount you have is limited.
3.		To be accurate, correct in your predictions
4.		A waste of money
5.		To spend money very quickly and carelessly
6.		Having money gives a person power and influence.

What would you do to find your dream job? In this blog entry and in the short documentary in the following Watching section, Sean Aiken searches for happiness and passion, not just a salary.

Circle the answer in the first or second column that best represents your philosophy about money, work, and happiness before you read the text. Compare your answers with a partner's.

Your Philosophy	
a. I want to have a job that I am passionate about.	**b.** The only reason to work is to pay the bills.
a. I will probably try many different jobs before finding the one I am passionate about.	**b.** I will probably stay in the first job I find after graduation.
a. I am willing to make less money if I am happy with my job.	**b.** I want to have the best-paying job possible, even if I don't love what I do.
a. I am willing to relocate if the job makes me happy.	**b.** I want to work close to home.

Read this excerpt from Sean's blog before watching his wacky adventure.

My Generation

By Sean Aiken

www.oneweekjob.com

My generation has been described as a "Peter Pan generation," "adultescents," "kidults," and by a host of other terms to describe how we are putting
5 off the transition into adulthood later than previous generations; generally taking longer to finish university, get married, move out, start a family, and enter the workforce.

If you asked me when I was ten, I
10 probably would have told you that I would be expecting my second child by now. But hey, times have changed, and so have we.

I think that many in my generation have seen our parents stuck doing the same
15 job they were not necessarily happy with for way too long. It's incredible how our careers play such an integral part of our lives: we tend to associate so much of our existence with them. Ask somebody to tell you about
20 themselves, and the majority will probably respond by first telling you what they do for a living.

If it is a fact that we spend most of our waking hours each day working, why not

>>

25 spend that time doing something we enjoy doing and are truly passionate about?

I think my generation is realizing this and sees the importance of making a career choice that suits our skill set and matches 30 our personality, values, and passions as well.

We have been told our whole life that anything is possible. Well, our parents did a great job, because now we actually believe it! The fact that we also live in an ever-shrinking 35 world with endless possibilities and a vast amount of choice can quickly become overwhelming.

I am positive I am not the only one kept up at night thinking, "Wow, what am I 40 going to do with my life?" Here we are with our entire lives before us. What path will we choose? Where will we end up?

I am scared, yet extremely excited and confident at the same time.

45 It takes a lot of courage to put yourself out there with an uncertain future ahead, and I am sure we all know the associated feeling very well, whether it resulted from a career decision, a relationship, moving out of your 50 parents' house, taking that trip around the world, or any other situation that required you to step out of your comfort zone.

It is a leap many are not willing to take and so they end up choosing to settle 55 into comfortable secure positions that they may or may not be happy with. Yet, it is in situations of uncertainty that we grow and learn the most about ourselves. And hey, if it doesn't work out as planned, life will 60 often give us a second chance.

And so here we go, I am taking a leap. Follow along with me on my journey and we will find out where it leads!

—Sean

476 words

Comprehension

1. How does Sean describe his generation, and why?

_____

_____

_____

2. When choosing a career, how is Sean's generation different from his parents'?

_____

_____

_____

3. What keeps Sean, and others of his generation, up at night? Do you share these worries?

_____

_____

_____

4. Sean talks about taking a leap. What leap is he talking about? What rewards await us if we do take the leap?

_____

_____

_____

_____

⟨0⟩ **WATCHING** One-Week Job

Learn more about Sean's journey by watching his documentary.

Comprehension

Read the questions. Then watch the video and answer them.

1. Fill in the blanks based on what you saw in the video.

   One man in search of _____ ᵃ, Sean Aiken travelled North America,

   working 52 _____ ᵇ in 52 _____ ᶜ, hoping to find his

   _____ ᵈ.

2. What diploma did Sean graduate with?

   _____

3. Did Sean have a career-plan for after his graduation? Explain your answer.

   _____

4. What advice does Sean's father give him? Does he take this advice?

   _____

   _____

5. What is the concept of the "one-week job"? Explain your answer.

   _____

   _____

6. What does Sean do with the money he makes?

   _____

7. Which jobs does Sean do during his "one-week job" experience? In the chart below, write down eight of the jobs shown in the video. Explain why you *would* or *would not* want to try each of the jobs listed.

Job	Reasons to Try or Not to Try
a.	
b.	
c.	
d.	
e.	
f.	
g.	
h.	

8. What does Sean learn by doing "one-week jobs"?

_____

_____

9. Fill in the blanks in the following text.

Now that my _____ [a] is over, I realize that finding a _____ [b]

is a continual process. What makes me _____ [c] today is not

necessarily the same thing that will make me happy five years down the road. For

now, my passion is to _____ [d] others to find their own.

📖 ▸ **READING** ▸ **FOR STRATEGY · ANNOTATING A TEXT**

A brand new car, an exotic vacation, the latest must-have gadget. What does it take
to make us happy? A recent study reveals that happiness might just be a question of
attitude.

Rate these items on a scale from 1 (most likely to bring you happiness) to
8 (least likely), before you read the article. Compare your ratings with a partner's.

_____ an interesting job   _____ free time

_____ the weather   _____ a luxury car

_____ good health   _____ friendships

_____ your education   _____ the latest electronic gadgets

FYI

WHAT MAKES THE GOOD LIFE

When asked what gives them
the most pleasure, people
favour health and home over
stuff:

Good health	84%
Owning your home	60%
Children	48%
Interesting job	46%
Free time	36%
Yard or garden	22%
Luxury or second car	19%
Latest electronic gadget	19%

_Happiness Study, based on the
Roper Reports Worldwide survey
published by GfK NOP_

Vocabulary

Find the words or expressions in bold in the article that match the following definitions.

1. to accomplish (v.)	
2. joining a trend (exp.)	
3. extremely happy, ecstatic (adj.)	
4. a state of mind or emotion (n.)	
5. to prosper (v.)	
6. thankfulness and appreciation (n.)	
7. depression or melancholy (n.)	
8. people of equal social standing and age (n.)	
9. thoughtfulness, generosity (n.)	
10. the opposite of a smile (n.)	

Annotating a Text

Read the article closely and annotate it according to the instructions in the How To.

The Way to Happiness

Proven tips to help you feel content with yourself and your life

By Dianne Hales
Reader's Digest

Everyone seems to be **jumping on the** get-happier **bandwagon**. Happiness is making **headlines**, selling books, inspiring scientific studies, and creating laughter clubs and joyology workshops. The reason? As the growing field of positive psychology has shown, happy people **thrive**. They're more creative and productive, earn more money, attract more friends, enjoy better marriages, stay healthier, and even **outlive** their unhappy **peers.**

"Imagine a drug that causes you to live eight or nine years longer, make $15 000 more a year, be less likely to get divorced," says Martin Seligman, PhD, who started the positive psychology movement almost a decade ago. "Happiness seems to be that drug."

But others wonder if this is just one more thing we feel pressured to **achieve** in our overscheduled lives? How could there be one path to happiness for all people? And if we aren't feeling **blissful**, are we **failures** at happiness?

Genetics, as research on 4000 sets of twins has demonstrated, accounts for about 50 per cent of your happiness quotient. But even if you inherited the family **frown** instead of joy genes, you're not fated to a life of **gloom**. Unless you're extremely poor or gravely **ill**, life circumstances account for only about 10 per cent of happiness. The other 40 per cent depends on what you do to make yourself happy.

Most of us assume that external things—a bigger house, a better job, a winning lottery ticket—will improve our lives. While they do bring temporary happiness, the thrill will fade. Happiness is like weight loss. We all know how to take off a few kilos; the trick is maintaining it.

In their research, psychologist Sonja Lyubomirsky, PhD, and her colleagues found that the key to **enduring** joy is to look beyond little pleasures, to the other aspects of what Seligman calls authentic happiness: engagement with family, work, or a passionate pursuit, and finding meaning from some higher purpose. "Different methods are better for different people," Lyubomirsky explains. "Keeping a daily **gratitude** journal, writing a letter of gratitude may be very meaningful." Timing and "doses" also matter. Performing five acts of **kindness** on one day, she found, gave a significant increase in well-being, while acts of kindness on different days didn't. "To **sustain** happiness," she emphasizes, "you have to make the effort and commitment every day for the rest of your life."

The long run generally brings greater contentment, according to studies that chart the trajectory of happiness over a lifetime. After even the most joyous childhood, happiness typically **declines** in the teens through the early 20s, but, believe it or not, increases as we age. "Young people tend to pay more attention to the bad," explains neuropsychologist Stacey Wood.

In fact, some experts say, happiness seems to rise even into old age. "Older adults don't react as intensely to life events,

How To

ANNOTATE A TEXT

To annotate is to make notes directly on a text as you read. Annotating allows the reader to pay close attention to a text and directly interact with it.

1. Underline the author's main point.

2. Double underline each new idea the author makes in developing the text. Write "idea 1," "idea 2," and so on, in the margin.

3. Put an asterisk next to major supporting sentences for ideas like statistics, personal anecdotes, and arguments.

4. Circle words that you do not understand.

5. Put a question mark next to ideas that are unclear or confusing.

6. Put an exclamation point next to passages that you strongly agree or disagree with, or that you find interesting.

headlines (n.) → most important items of news

outlive (v.) → live longer than

enduring (adj.) → lasting

sustain (v.) → maintain

failures (n.) → unsuccessful people

declines (v.) → decreases

ill (adj.) → sick

Listen to "The Science of Happiness" online to learn more about the pursuit of happiness from the point of view of evolution.

spirit (n.) → mental quality

75 and they report fewer negative emotions and more positive ones," says Wood.

Regardless of your age or temperament, you can feel happier right this minute, claims psychologist Will Fleeson, PhD, of Wake Forest University, who says he has 80 found a strategy to increase the **spirit**: do something, however small, that is energetic, adventurous, assertive, or bold. When volunteers recorded their feelings throughout the day, all felt happier when 85 active and engaged.

"The biggest surprise in this research was that you can change your behaviour and make yourself feel happier easily," says Fleeson, who found that almost any active 90 behaviour—even singing or dancing to the radio—has a positive effect on **mood.** "Laughing out loud is exactly the kind of adventurous bold action that makes you feel happier."

724 words

Fill in the chart below by referring to your annotation of the article.

The Main Idea of the Text	Words You Do Not Understand and Their Definition	Confusing or Unclear Ideas	Ideas That You Strongly Agree or Disagree with

Comprehension

1. What advantages do happy people have?

_____

_____

2. Our happiness quotient is divided up into three parts. What are these parts?

_____

_____

3. Why will a bigger house not bring lasting happiness?

_____

_____

4. What is authentic happiness?

_____

_____

5. At what age does happiness typically decrease? Why?

_____

_____

6. What can you do to feel happier right now?

_____

_____

_____

Focus on Language: Modals

▷ **Refer to Grammar Link, page 115, for more infomation on modals.**

1. Read the following excerpts from the article. Underline each modal and indicate its function or meaning.

a. How could there be one path to happiness for all people? _____

b. Keeping a daily gratitude journal may be very meaningful. _____

c. . . . you can feel happier right this minute. _____

Discussion

1. When you are in a bad mood or feel gloomy, what do you do to feel happy?

2. Does going out to socialize or to party make you feel happy? Explain your answer.

3. Is our generation too focused on feeling happy? What would be a better use of our time and energy?

 **SPEAKING** Laughter Quiz

Read "The Science of Fun" online to find out more about why we need to have fun.

Can the physical act of laughing improve your life?

Take the laughter quiz and discuss your answers with a partner.

1. How often do you laugh?
   a. often
   b. sometimes
   c. rarely
   d. never

2. In which situation are you most likely to laugh?
   a. when someone tells a good joke
   b. when you watch a funny movie
   c. when you see someone else laugh
   d. when you are doing something fun

3. Do you think laughter has a positive impact on your health?

   a. yes   **b.** no   **c.** I don't know

4. If you answered *yes* to question 3, what are the benefits of laughter on your health? Circle all the answers that apply.

   a. reduces my stress levels   **d.** reduces physical pain

   b. helps me relax   **e.** makes me happier

   c. puts me in a better mood

5. Are we born to laugh?

   a. yes   **b.** no

6. Who do you think laughs more? Explain your answer.

   a. young children   **c.** parents

   b. teenagers   **d.** grandparents

7. Why do you think people stop laughing? Circle all the answers that apply.

   a. too much stress in their life   **c.** think it is childish

   b. too busy   **d.** forget how

8. What do you think *laughercize* means?

   a. laughing while you exercise

   b. laughing to lose weight

   c. a laughing exercise program led by a laughologist

   d. a smiling program to improve facial muscles

◄(O)► WATCHING Laughter Is the Best Medicine

Can you laugh your way to a better life? Watch this CTV news report to find out more about the benefits of laughter.

Vocabulary

Match each word or expression with its correct definition before you watch the video.

1.	open-minded (adj.)		**a.** to succeed, yield good results
2.	to be in stitches (exp.)		**b.** sick
3.	side effect (n.)		**c.** receptive to new and different ideas
4.	a winning edge (exp.)		**d.** a secondary consequence
5.	ill (adj.)		**e.** a competitive advantage
6.	to fake it (v.)		**f.** to take a situation less seriously
7.	to pay off (v.)		**g.** to laugh so hard that you have a pain in your side
8.	to lighten up (exp.)		**h.** to pretend

Comprehension

Read the questions. Then watch the video and answer them.

1. Fill in the blanks with the missing words.

   Can the physical act of _____[a] really beat _____[b] and manage pain?

2. Why did Morgan stop laughing? Where and how did he learn to laugh again?

   _____

   _____

3. How long does it take for the fake laughter to turn into real laughter?

   _____

   _____

4. How do we lose our laughter?

   _____

   _____

5. What are the negative effects of not laughing?

   _____

   _____

6. What is Dr. Pineau studying? What does he hope to find?

   _____

   _____

7. What are the benefits of laughter therapy in the health field?

   _____

   _____

8. What are the benefits of laughter therapy for elementary students?

   _____

   _____

9. Return to the Laughter Quiz on page 127. Correct your answers based on what the experts explained in this news report.

Topic Files

Topic Files Topic Files Topic File

Write a text or give an oral presentation on one of the following topics. Try to incorporate the elements seen in the unit from the Make the Connection box and use as many of the Top Words as you can, where appropriate.

Make the Connection

- ☐ Modals
- ☐ Vocabulary and idioms from the unit
- ☐ Pronouncing *can* versus *can't*
- ☐ Annotating a text
- ☐ Writing an argumentative essay

▷ Refer to Writing Files 2, page 65, for information about essays.

▷ Refer to appendix 1, page 155, for information about oral presentations.

1 CAN MONEY BUY HAPPINESS?: Do material possessions like cars, jewellery, and gadgets, make us happier? What is the link between our happiness and our spending habits?

2 ONE WEEK JOBS: How important is it to find a job we love and are passionate about? Should we all have a job we love?

3 HAPPY COUNTRIES: Which country do you think is the happiest? Lots of research has been done in the past decade to find out who the happiest people on the planet are and why. Research this topic to find out more.

4 LAUGHOLOGY: What are the benefits of laughter on our health and well-being? Research laughology to find out more.

5 PARTY ANIMALS: Why do we need to have fun? Is it important to our survival? Go to Chenelière Interactive and read the article "The Science of Fun" to find out more.

6 OTHER: _____ Write about another topic of your choice linked to what you learned in this unit. Make sure to have your topic approved by your teacher.

Top Words

Put a check mark next to the words you know and refer to the page numbers to learn the ones you don't know. Add to the list other words that you want to remember from the unit.

ADJECTIVES

- ☐ blissful (124)
- ☐ open-minded (128)

EXPRESSIONS

- ☐ in the long run (118)
- ☐ to fake it (128)
- ☐ to lighten up (128)

NOUNS

- ☐ bonding (118)
- ☐ charity (117)
- ☐ a frown (124)
- ☐ gloom (124)
- ☐ gratitude (124)
- ☐ income (117)
- ☐ kindness (124)
- ☐ mood (124)
- ☐ peers (124)
- ☐ a purchase (118)

VERBS

- ☐ to achieve (124)
- ☐ to earn (117)
- ☐ to fade (118)
- ☐ to spend (117)
- ☐ to thrive (124)

OTHER:

_____ _____

_____ _____

_____ _____

_____ _____

Vocabulary from the unit and other theme-related vocabulary can be practised online.

Are You Under the Influence?

The impact advertisement and marketing campaigns have on you

> Are marketing companies secretly watching or tracking you?

> What clever strategies are marketers using to target your generation?

> Are marketers using certain colours to influence you to buy?

In this unit you will explore how marketing and advertising influence what we buy and how we view ourselves and the world.

WORD OF MOUTH

Famous Slogans

branding (n.) → a unique name and image that identify a product in consumers' minds

FYI

7UP
Apple
Coca-Cola
Energizer
Nike
Subway
Volkswagen

Positive Slogan and Brand Qualities

catchy	informative
clever	interesting
colourful	luxurious
cool	memorable
cute	powerful
fashionable	reliable
funny	sexy
good value	stylish
humorous	timeless
in style	well-made

Negative Slogan and Brand Qualities

boring	overused
childish	poor quality
in bad taste	pretentious
old-fashioned	tacky
out of style	unreliable

A company's **branding** starts with a slogan. The best slogans become part of our everyday speech. What decisions do you make about a brand based on its slogan?

Work with a partner to complete the chart below. The brands are listed in the blue margin box. Use the adjectives in the orange margin box to describe the qualities associated with each slogan and brand.

Slogan/Brand	What products do they sell?	What is the message of the slogan?	What qualities do you associate with the brand and slogan?
1. Just Do It. Nike	Sportswear and shoes	Powerful and encouraging	Well-made, powerful, and stylish
2. Think different. Apple	Eletronics.	Be different	Cool and catchy clever
3. Das Auto. Volkswagen	Cars	Cheap car/ Popular Quality	timeless good value
4. The Uncola 7up	Soda/drinks	Irony with coca-cola. Different.	Pretentious
5. Open Happiness Coca-cola	Soda.	Be happy with coca-cola.	timeless cute memorable.
6. Eat Fresh. Subway.	Sandwich	Eat good/ healthy	Good value.
7. Keep going and going. Energizer	Batteries.	Durability good value humorous	Powerful. humorous.
8. Your favourite slogan/brand: Nike	Sportswear and shoes.		

Discussion

1. Do you think you choose a particular product based on the company's logo and slogan? Explain your answer.

2. Explain how you would react in the following hypothetical situations. Use the conditional form to express yourself.

   If I see an ad for something tasty when I am hungry . . .
   If ads were against the law . . .
   If I were able to create ads for my generation . . .
   If I had invested in Apple stocks many years ago . . .

📖 **READING   FOR INTERACTION**

Do you know how far some marketers go to get you to buy their products? What type of marketing does your generation, known as the Millennial generation, respond to?

Decide if these statements about the Millennials and the marketing aimed at them are true or false before you read the article. Discuss your thoughts with a partner. Then read the article to verify your answers. If the statement is false, write the correct statement on the line provided.

1. Millennials were born between 1970–2010.   T   F

2. Millennials make up 20% of the population.   T   F

3. Millennials buy fewer packaged goods than baby boomers.   T   F

4. Marketers must use social networks to reach Millennials.   T   F

5. Word-of-mouth marketing is very important to Millennials.   T   F

6. Millennials respond to honest marketing messages.   T   F

7. Most Millennials buy products from any company that offers a good price. T   F

8. Millennials rely on parents' opinions when buying a product.   T   F

Grammar Link

CONDITIONALS

Use the conditional form to express possible, improbable, or impossible situations in the present, future, or past.

Future possible conditionals
*If I **see** running shoes on sale, I **will buy** a pair.*

Present improbable and unreal conditionals
*If I **had** more money, I **would buy** more electronic gadgets.*

Impossible conditionals
*If I **had** watched less television in high school, I **would have been** less influenced by all that advertising.*

▶ Refer to *REAL Grammar Book 2*, unit 9, for more information on conditionals.

Marketing to Millennials

By Ripley Daniels

Today's **marketers** must be very **aware** of a new breed of consumer born between 1980 and 2000. These "deciders" make up 20 percent of the global population. Known as Echo Boomers or Millennials, they've **grown up** in the digital world where cellphones, text messaging, and envelope-thin laptops are *de rigueur* for survival. If you're marketing anything
5 to them, you'd better know as much as you can about them, for their buying habits can make the difference between the success and failure of your business.

Millennials are diverse, highly educated, and solidly influential **shoppers**. They are more ethnically, economically, and socially diverse than any previous consuming generation. They also spend freely. They buy more consumer packaged goods (items that need to be replaced
10 frequently) than **baby boomers**.

The omnipresence and power of digital devices allow Millennials to connect with each other like no other demographic ever has, comparing, advising, **praising**, and, yes, **bad mouthing** products and services in increasingly public forums. Loyalties are begun "on the street" with these young consumers. Forget sterile **focus groups** and other traditional
15 **advertising** approaches. The new place to measure a product's impact is on social networks. Fail here and your product is **history**.

A Millennial's brand loyalty comes from real product trials and **word-of-mouth** reviews. Opinions multiply on social media sites like Facebook, YouTube, Pinterest, and others. Online user-generated feedback in the form of product reviews, personal Q&As, and shared
20 experiences have more of an impact than the **brand** messaging of traditional advertisers.

With Millennials, you have to be honest, for it's all about **trust** and **backing up** what you say. That means every **slogan**, every promise, every "**stat** you cite" had better be real and measurable. To these **buyers**, you don't have to be the **cheapest**, or even the most popular, but you have to deliver on the spirit of your promise—or face the Fury of Facebook, the
25 Punishment of Pinterest, or a crushing cascade of negative tweets. And that can happen faster than a 13-year-old can text, "This sucks!"

While product quality and delivering on a promise are important, if you market a product to Millennials, you must have a conscience. A Pew Research survey revealed that 34 percent of Millennials bought a certain product or service because of a company's social or political **values**.
30 When the line between different or competing **products** begins to **blur**, Millennials rely on the opinions of their **peers**—on company sites as well as social media. Markets most influenced by the impact of user-generated content include electronics, cars and trucks, hotel stays, travel, and insurance. Unlike their parents, Millennials are no longer influenced by brand messages. It is understandable when you consider that this breed of consumer has seen
35 more advertising than any generation in the history of consumption.

So how do you make human contact with Millennials? First, you must find ways to include yourself in their conversations. To do that, you'll need to locate today's ever-fluid media to deliver their message—be it online, in-store, or, increasingly, via mobile devices. You must also learn the language of Millennials, or **be shut out** as mere "**pitchmen**." And you must really listen to
40 what's being said about you and your products, and be willing to adapt to changing consumer needs. Finally, you must have a social conscience—be it "green," animal rights, or human rights.

The Millennials are out there and growing. They have money. The media they communicate with and messages they respond to are different (and often smarter) than you might expect.

589 words

history (exp.) → irrelevant

stat (n.) → abbreviation of *statistic*

blur (n.) → become unclear

pitchmen (n.) → advertising executives

Vocabulary

Work with a partner and read the word clues to find the words or expressions to complete the crossword puzzle.
Hint: All of the answers are in bold in the article on the previous page.

Across

5. people born between 1946-1964
6. expressing approval or admiration
7. speaking badly of something
10. informed of current developments
13. classmates or people in your age group
14. communicated orally
15. people who go to stores to buy products
17. people who purchase products
18. merchandise
19. be excluded

Down

1. the promotion of goods or services for sale through the media
2. supporting or reinforcing
3. become adult
4. people brought together to give their opinions on a particular issue or product
7. trademark or distinctive name identifying a product or a manufacturer
8. people who promote and sell goods or services
9. ideas about what is important
11. confidence in
12. least expensive
16. phrase used repeatedly in advertising or promotion

Marketing

How important is word-of-mouth advertising to your generation? Learn some common idiomatic expressions people often use when they talk about marketing and advertising.

Complete each idiomatic expression with a verb from the word box. Study the meaning of each idiom.

to create	to run
to drum up	to seal
to get	to sell
to plug	to throw

Idiom	Meaning
1. _____ a product	to promote or talk positively about a product
2. _____ an ad	to place an advertisement in the media
3. _____ down to business	to get serious; to begin to negotiate or conduct business
4. _____ money at	to try to solve a problem by spending a lot of money on it
5. _____ like hotcakes	to sell very quickly and in large numbers
6. _____ the deal	to finalize an agreement
7. _____ a buzz	to generate hype or excitement
8. _____ business	to try to make people buy something

Read the following dialogue and fill in the blanks with the correct idiomatic expressions. Then role-play the dialogue with a partner and practise using the idiomatic expressions correctly.

Edward and Erica work for a marketing company. They are having a business lunch in a sports bar and discussing an upcoming ad campaign proposal they are working on together.

Edward: Hey Erica, did you watch the hockey game last night?

Erica: I had the TV on, but I was actually thinking about this campaign. We should _____[1] right away. We have a very tight deadline.

Edward: Whatever you say. You're the boss!

Erica: Let's begin by brainstorming some ways we can _____[2]. How can we get the Millennials to talk positively about this new energy bar?

Edward: We have to remember that the client doesn't want to spend a lot of money. We need an inexpensive way to _____[3] and attention around the product in order to _____[4]. This will be challenging. Hmmm. Do you have any brilliant ideas?

Erica: Well, since we can't _____[5] this one, we could _____[6] on the social network sites young people use these days.

>>

Edward: Yes! That's a cheap and effective way to reach a lot of people. We could even give away free samples of the new energy bars in exchange for a "liked" page.

Erica: Great idea! We'll let those kids spread the word for us. Before we know it, the bars will begin to _____7. Everyone will want them.

Edward: Do you think the client will approve the campaign?

Erica: I'll submit this in writing and with luck we'll be able to _____8 later this week.

Edward: I hope so. I'd hate to see you miss too many more hockey games!

 **SPEAKING** # Talk About Advertising

You have been chosen to attend a youth focus-group meeting. In this meeting, you will discuss effective marketing strategies that **target** your generation.

target → aim at

Your Ad Here

Prepare for the meeting by doing the following:

1. Find a commercial that caught your attention and left a strong impression on you. It can be from the Internet or television.

2. Describe the commercial or show it to a small group of students.

3. As you describe the commercial

   • Use the simple past and the past progressive.

   I saw a really memorable commercial earlier this month for Google Glass. In this commercial two people were skydiving and taking pictures of their free fall with their glasses. It was really interesting and innovative . . .

   • Use the brand and slogan qualities vocabulary from the box on page 132 to help you explain what you liked about the ad and the impact it had on you.

   • Did this ad encourage you to use or purchase the product? Explain your answer.

   • Comment on the effectiveness of this commercial. Try to incorporate an idiom from the above activity into your answer.

Marketing Vocabulary

To effectively discuss marketing and the influence advertisers have on us, you need to know the difference between these words.

To advertise (v.) is to present or provide information about products or services in order to encourage sales

An advertisement (n.) is any text, image, or short film in a newspaper, on a billboard, on television, on radio, or online, designed to sell products and services

▶ *Did you see the new advertisement for the latest Apple gadget?*

An ad (n.) is an abbreviation of *advertisement*

A commercial (n.) is an advertisement on television or radio

▶ *Advertisers spend millions of dollars on the commercials shown during the television broadcast of the Superbowl.*

Publicity (n.) is the act of promoting or advertising a product

▶ *The advertisement is part of McDonald's new publicity campaign.*

Pronunciation

Numbers

Part 1: Identifying and Using Cardinal and Ordinal Numbers

Cardinal numbers (1, 2, 3, 4, 5) are used to describe quantity.

Ordinal numbers (1st *first*, 2nd *second*, 3rd *third*, 4th *fourth*, 5th *fifth*) are used to describe position, rank, and dates. Be sure to pronounce the /th/ sound correctly as you say the ordinal numbers.

Listen to these tongue twisters and repeat what you hear. Then say them as quickly as you can.

One-one was a race horse. Two-two was one too. One-one won one race. Two-two won one too.

Thirty-three thirsty, thundering thoroughbreds thumped Mr. Thurber on Thursday.

Listen to the following sentences and circle the cardinal or ordinal number you hear. Then repeat it after the speaker.

1. 4	4th	14th	40	**4.** 7	17th	7th	17
2. 16	16th	60	6th	**5.** 9	19	90	90th
3. 13	13th	3rd	30	**6.** 80th	80	18th	18

Part 2: Saying Big Numbers Correctly

Look at this number: 56 744 111. Can you say it?

Break it down as follows:

56 – fifty six million
     744 – seven hundred and forty-four thousand
         111 – one hundred and eleven

When you say large numbers, do not make hundred, thousand, or million plural. (*twenty thousands dollars, seven millions people*)

Use spaces to separate thousands, millions, etc. (21 067).

You will often hear *a* instead of *one* before hundred, thousand, etc. and *and* before the last number (*a hundred and twenty-five*).

Listen to the following sentences and write down the number you hear. Use numerals and not words.

1. _____   3. _____   5. _____

2. _____   4. _____   6. _____

Create four sentences on a separate piece of paper that contain a mix of ordinal, cardinal, and big numbers.

Dictate your sentences to your partner and then listen to his or her sentences. Write the numbers you hear on a separate piece of paper. Compare your numbers with your partner's original sentence. Did you get the number right?

Pay careful attention to the many numbers in the documentary that follows.

⟨●⟩ WATCHING Hunting for Cool

Millennials don't respond to traditional brand-marketing messages. They respond to what's "cool." This PBS program takes a look at how corporate marketing "culture spies" track trendsetting teens to discover what's cool.

Vocabulary

Watch the introduction to the video, and fill in the blanks with the missing words. Be sure you understand the meaning of these words before you watch the rest of the video.

1. They want to be _____. They are _____, and they have the

   _____.

2. They are corporate America's _____ dream. _____ have a

   lot of _____.

3. MTV, Madison Avenue, and the dream-makers of Hollywood have _____

   our teenagers.

4. If you don't understand and _____ what they are thinking and what they

   are feeling, you are going to _____.

5. But what does this _____ focus on the teenager do to the _____?

Comprehension

Read the questions. Then watch the rest of the video and answer them.

The Focus-Group Meeting

1. Where does the focus-group meeting take place?

   _____

2. What do the market researchers want the boys to tell them?

   _____

3. How much money do the boys make to participate in the focus group?

   _____

Facts and Statistics

4. How many teens are there in the United States? _____

5. How much money did teens spend in one year? _____

6. How much money did teens get their parents to spend on them?

   _____

7. How many ads does a typical teen process every day? _____

8. How many ads will teens have processed by the time they are 18 years old?

_____

9. How many teens have a television in their bedroom? _____

10. How many teens have a personal computer? _____

11. On average, how many hours do teens spend online every day? _____

"Coolhunting"

12. How do marketers 'win' teen loyalty?

_____

_____

13. What makes this age group so frustrating to marketers?

_____

14. What is one thing this age group does respond well to? _____

15. When marketers go "coolhunting," what are they looking for?

_____

_____

16. Who is Dee Dee Gordon?

_____

17. What do correspondents or "culture spies" do?

_____

18. How much do companies have to pay for a subscription to the Look-Look website?

_____

19. Why would companies want to know what the next cool trend will be?

_____

_____

20. What is the paradox of coolhunting?

_____

Apple	McDonald's
Facebook	Microsoft
GAP	Starbucks
Kraft	Virgin Mobile
Your choice: _____	

▶ See Writing Files 2 and 3, pages 65 and 109, for more information on essay writing, thesis statements, introductions, and conclusions.

Writing

Write a short argumentative essay about how you think big companies influence youth to buy or use their product or service. Look in the margin box for some big companies to choose from. Explain if you think their marketing strategies are effective or ineffective.

• Write a clear thesis statement and give adequate support.

• Limit your essay topic by focusing on one big company.

• Do research and analyze the company's current or recent advertising campaign. Explain how its advertisments are designed to appeal to young people.

SPEAKING # Think Before You Pink

Every year, millions of dollars are spent on items with pink ribbons or green logos, thanks to *cause advertising*. It can be very successful if it is done properly.

Work with a partner to think critically about the images and slogans for the following fictitious advertising campaigns. Answer the questions in the chart below. Can you see any irony, problems, or conflicts of interest in these campaigns?

The Slogan and the Image	The Product and the Cause	What is the link between the product and the cause?	Do you think this ad campaign is effective in helping the cause?
1. Drive on air	Product: _____ Cause: _____	_____ _____ _____ _____	☐ Yes ☐ No Why: _____ _____ _____
2. Nature's Best	Product: _____ Cause: _____	_____ _____ _____ _____	☐ Yes ☐ No Why: _____ _____ _____
3. The Beauty of a Cure	Product: _____ Cause: _____	_____ _____ _____ _____	☐ Yes ☐ No Why: _____ _____ _____
4. Natural Baby, Happy Baby	Product: _____ Cause: _____	_____ _____ _____ _____	☐ Yes ☐ No Why: _____ _____ _____

How To

THINK CRITICALLY

Critical thinking is a skill you should use every day. It helps you to form educated and informed opinions about what you learn in the classroom or find in the media.

A good critical thinker does not accept information at face value but questions, analyzes, and evaluates new information.

To think critically about a situation you need to ask yourself the following questions:

- Who benefits from this information?
- How recent is this information?
- Who published this information?
- What is the author's or publisher's purpose in this text or situation? Is it to inform, persuade, or entertain me?

Read "Fair Trade: An Alternative Economic Model" online to learn about another important cause marketing campaign.

Breast Cancer Action Montréal is speaking out against "pink-washing." Read the article to learn more about who benefits the most from cause marketing and what you can do to make a difference.

Pink Ribbon Green

By Dan Delmar
Special to *The Suburban*

fundraising (v.) → collecting money for a cause

bottom line (n.) → profits

I t's a common scene in many Montréal workplaces: A benevolent co-worker frantically **1** tries to get every last cent out of colleagues in order to meet a **fundraising** goal for a pink ribbon charity. These efforts may be helping a good cause, but what many don't realize is that they're also helping to boost someone's **bottom line**.

5   Money is being made from events like the Weekend to End Breast Cancer either directly, **2** by the organizer who is paid to coordinate and promote the event, or indirectly, by companies whose brand is bolstered because of their association with a charity. Not that there is anything inherently wrong with compensation for organizing good works, but organizations need to ensure that the charity's main goal—collecting funds for a worthy cause—is respected.

10   "Breast cancer affects everyone," explained Madeleine Bird, a Project Coordinator with Breast **3** Cancer Action Montréal (BCAM) and McGill's Centre for Research and Teaching on Women. "It strikes randomly at people who society views as vulnerable: mothers, grandmothers, aunts, etc."And, as is the case with many other forms of advertising, sex sells. "Breasts are very attractive and sexy," Bird said. "They nurture us." It's no wonder that pink ribbons are found on many products, from

hypocrisy (n.) → falseness

rising (v.) → increasing

15 automobiles to yogurt. Bird says there's an underlying **hypocrisy** when corporations like the Ford Motor Company plaster the pink ribbon on the same SUVs whose emissions are contributing to **rising** cancer rates. Cosmetic products, which are primarily targeted at women, in some cases, contain chemicals known as parabens which have been linked to breast cancer. Parabens are preservatives used in cosmetics to prolong shelf life. Although no definitive connection has been found between

20 them and cancer, they are known to mimic estrogen in the body and have been found in the tissue of breast tumours. Despite this, Bird says companies like Avon or Ultramar would rather associate themselves with the battle against breast cancer, as opposed to diseases which aren't as "sexy."

trend (n.) → tendency

funds (n.) → money

   From a marketing standpoint, it's a "win-win situation," according to Robert Soroka, **4** professor of marketing at Dawson College. The industry refers to this **trend** as 'Cause
25 Marketing.' It helps marketers foster positive attitudes toward their products in the minds of consumers while providing much needed **funds** to a worthy charity.

   The "pink-washing," as it's been called, began in the early 1990s as a grassroots campaign. **5** Charlotte Haley, an American woman who watched her daughter, grandmother, and sister all fight breast cancer, petitioned the National Cancer Institute to invest more in prevention.
30 She mailed peach-coloured ribbons with her messages of protest and, soon after, the idea was adopted by cosmetics giant Estée Lauder and *Self Magazine*. Through research and focus groups, it was determined that pink ribbons were more consumer-friendly because pink symbolized warmth and femininity.   **>>**

"The pink ribbon itself is corporate," Bird said. Nonetheless, charities tend to "not [6]
35 bite the hand that feeds them," she said. That seems to be the case at the Jewish General
Hospital as well where Beverley Kravitz, the Director of Planned Giving, said it makes sense
to **hand over** roughly 30 percent of money raised to CauseForce—a for-profit company.   **hand over** (v.) → give
That's because organizing and marketing an event the size of the Weekend to End Breast
Cancer simply couldn't be done without outside help. "An awareness campaign is incredibly
40 important," Kravitz said. "We couldn't handle it on our own." The return-on-investment is
also substantially larger than with most other charity events.

The event poses a challenge for volunteer fundraisers, however. Those who don't **raise** [7]   **raise** (v.) → collect
a minimum of $2 000 are not permitted to take part in the walk. It's meant to be a motivator,
according to a CauseForce spokesperson who spoke with *The Suburban*. "I don't know if I
45 would be able to raise that much with my friends," Bird said. "It limits the demographic of
people that can participate."

One alternative proposed by BCAM President Carol Secter is to skip the middleman and [8]
donate directly to the Segal Cancer Centre, ensuring that no one will profit monetarily from   **donate** (v.) → contribute as a gift
a donation. "That would be money well spent," Sector said. "One could say, 'I won't walk. I'll
50 just write you a check for $200. I'll still get my receipt and the hospital will get all the money.'"

Like Haley, the mother of the peach ribbon, the women heading BCAM want more [9]
attention focused on how breast cancer could, not only be treated effectively, but stopped
from ever forming in the first place.

"Too much of it focuses on the individual actions of women (like the breast [10]
55 self-exam)," Bird said. "The efforts are good, but we should put more effort into finding
safer substitutes in the products we use every day." The message sent by the pink ribbon
is "keep consuming and everything is going to be fine. We can't buy our way out of the
problem but we're being sold that message," she said. "Think more critically instead of
jumping on the bandwagon."

821 words

Comprehension

1. What does "to boost someone's bottom line" mean in paragraph one? Whose
bottom line is being boosted?

_____

_____

2. According to the article, why are pink ribbons found on so many products?

_____

_____

3. Explain what is hypocritical about cosmetic companies that associate their product
with the pink ribbon?

_____

4. What is a win-win situation (paragraph four)? How does this relate to cause marketing?

_____

_____

5. Explain what "charities tend not to bite the hand that feeds them" means in
paragraph six?

_____

6. How did the "pink-washing" begin?

_____

_____

7. How much money do volunteers have to raise to be able to walk in the

fundraising event? _____

8. What message do the pink ribbon campaigns send? Is this a good message to send? Explain your answer.

_____

_____

Discussion

1. Have you or someone you know participated in a pink ribbon fundraising activity, or other charity events like this? Describe the experience.

2. Before you give to a cause, do you ask how much of your money will actually go to the cause?

3. Now that you understand the issues involved in cause marketing, return to the "Think Before You Pink" speaking activity on page 141 and see if you want to reconsider some of your answers in the third column.

 **LISTENING** # How Colour Makes Us Buy

Pink? Green? Did you know that colors have a secret language? A simple change in colour can affect the sales of a product immediately. Listen to Terry O' Reilly from CBC's "Under the Influence," as he explores how colours persuade us to buy.

FYI

CBC Radio host Terry O'Reilly has won national and international awards for writing and directing notable actors like Alec Baldwin, Ellen DeGeneres, Kiefer Sutherland, Bob Newhart, Martin Short, and Drew Carey.

Discussion

1. What is your favourite colour? What do you think this colour says about you?

2. What colour is your bedroom? Does the colour of your room have an effect on you? Explain your answer.

3. What colour is the sign for your favourite fast-food restaurant? Do you think this colour has an influence on you?

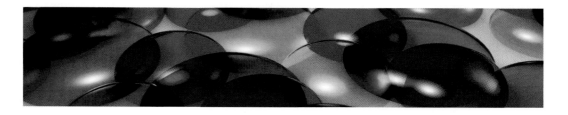

Comprehension

1. Listen to the radio show and take notes in the chart below.

	Meaning of Colour in Marketing	Companies that Use this Colour	Important Details About this Colour
RED	Passion, ation, fire, rebellion advent, best, courage angry	Brands (Virgin)	appeti.
BLUE	Securitia, trust, calm of mind producti	IBM UNIflag.	Most in the World, stay (history) in good hands. Motrola
ORANGE	Food Value, discounts	Bank Online	n/a
GREEN	Freshenem, enviro.	Subway	bonnew your self
PURPLE	Nobli, (wel) money	Queen Cap. Choco.	Queen Victoria. UK.
BROWN	Earth, honest, independ		18%
YELLOW	fun, opti., cheeriness	n/a	n/a
BLACK	Absence, power, lux, authorith	n/a	n/a
WHITE	innovation, lightness cleanlem	Apple	lightness

2. Explain why the McDonald's logo is yellow and red and not blue.

Estimulte appeti. fun. because not exist blue foods.

3. What is the best colour for an office space? Why?

Yellow / White.

4. Why is there a lot of red in Las Vegas?

5. Why did the coach paint the visiting team's locker room pink?

reduce tes aggression.

6. What colour makes men and women seem more attractive to each other? Why?

a. red   **b.** blue   **c.** green

physically respond instincts

7. How did these companies use colour in their marketing campaign and what result did it have?

Company	Colour Modification	Reason for Change	Result
a. Hot dog company	red		
b. Tidy Bowl			
c. Xerox	blue → red	action	

Discussion and Writing

Can you think of other examples of companies that are strongly associated with a particular colour? Based on the episode of "Under the Influence" that you listened to, why do you think they chose this colour?

📖 READING   FOR STRATEGY · SUMMARY WRITING

Do you shop online or research products on the Internet? What do you think this virtual activity says about you as a consumer? Read the article to find out more about how we are being tracked online.

Discuss these statements with a partner and decide if these statements are true or false before you read the article.

	True	False
1. Marketers buy personal information about you.		
2. If you are shopping on the Internet for a new car, or a vacation, Google knows this and shares this information with advertisers.		
3. Facebook monitors your conversations and sends targeted ads to you.		
4. Credit card companies judge you based on your purchases.		
5. People who buy cheap motor oil were more likely to miss a credit-card payment than those who bought more expensive oil.		
6. The "erosion of personal privacy" is a not a big concern for consumers.		

Vocabulary

Match each word or expression with its correct definition before you read. The line number is given in parentheses.

1. to track (v., 3)		**a.** to say
2. to figure out (v., 13)		**b.** indifferent
3. to hire (v., 14)		**c.** to employ
4. a fingerprint (n., 21)		**d.** to understand or discover
5. to tailor to (v., 50)		**e.** to observe or monitor
6. to utter (v., 71)		**f.** merit or value
7. worthiness (n., 78)		**g.** to make especially for someone
8. apathetic (adj., 108)		**h.** pattern of lines on bottom of end of finger

Hyper-Targeting: How Brands Track You Online

By Terry O'Reilly

Marketers are buying more and more personal [1] information about consumers. This information is then being used to track people online, as marketers watch their buying habits. As a result, advertisers are "hyper-targeting"
5 consumers with ads that are made for individuals, featuring the products they want, when they want them, at a price based on their spending ability, and at the precise moment they are about to make a choice. How did this happen?

When the Internet arrived in the early 90s, people [2]
10 moved online in search of content, but didn't want to pay for it. So online publishers did the only thing they could do— they looked to media buyers for survival. They knew if they could figure out who was visiting their websites, they could sell that information to advertisers. So they began to hire
15 companies that specialized in analyzing how many visitors were logging onto their sites, who they were, and where they were coming from. This became easier in 1994, when a computer programmer at Netscape came up with the idea of using electronic "cookies." Essentially, cookies were small text
20 files that assigned an identification code to the visitor. Like a fingerprint, it worked this way: The moment you logged onto a website, it automatically placed a cookie on your computer. And the next time you visited, the website recognized that cookie. Therefore, when you put several items into your shopping
25 cart, the website recognized all those purchases were made by the same person. That cookie also gave the website other information—like where you had clicked previously, what had been put in the cart but not purchased, what pages you had visited, and for how long.

30 The creators of the electronic cookie then made one other [3] important decision; to place the cookies on people's computers without asking permission. That decision would have lasting consequences. Companies like DoubleClick developed ways to use cookies to observe a visitor's behaviour and then send the same
35 person more ads for the same product on other pages across its 3000+ website network. In other words, it could track consumers.

Many online companies began to share and purchase [4] data about their registrants with and from other companies the registrants used. For example, an auto company might
40 purchase information about you from an airline you've dealt with—and learn your age, gender, marital status, ethnicity, profession, credit status, number of airline flights you've taken in the past 12 months, number of kids you have, their age ranges, and the value of your home. All of this is done without
45 your knowledge.

When that information is added to the past details [5] you provided when you registered on their site, a complete behavioural profile is created for you. With that, "hyper-targeting" begins. Hyper-targeting allows media planners to
50 send perfectly tailored ads directly to individuals, based on deep knowledge of that individual's personal life, at the exact moment they are about to buy something. For example, a car company has been quietly tracking you, and they see you've been on five different auto sites. It's obvious you're shopping

>>

for a new car. Since they've bought access to your credit information, they know you have the financial resources to buy a car. Then one morning they observe you visiting a vehicle-financing site. At this point, the car company would take advantage of hyper-targeting and place an ad on that website and offer you a discount on their car at the very moment you are about to arrange financing. That's hyper-targeting.

Facebook is another source of information for online **6** companies. It is able to monitor conversations to gather comments from users talking about brands. My wife was having a conversation with some girlfriends on Facebook about an upcoming wedding. Not long after, wedding-related ads started appearing on her home page. Facebook claims this monitoring is done by software and that no humans are reading your posts, but it's still another example of how companies collect data. Recently, Facebook started experimenting with monitoring conversations in real time. So if you uttered the line, "Boy, I could go for a pizza tonight" you would be served up a pizza ad or coupon instantly. It's every advertiser's dream.

There was a time when credit card companies were only **7** interested in making sure you kept up your payments. But now, they seem to be judging you on your purchases. Credit card companies routinely monitor our spending to create profiles to determine credit-worthiness. They look for signs of financial and personal problems. For example, if you begin using your credit card at second-hand stores, or when charges start appearing for marriage therapy, the credit card company will start watching you more closely. If you log in to your credit card balance at one in the morning, it will signal sleeplessness due to financial anxiety. If you check your balance three times a day, it will be a warning sign. By tracking your private purchases, companies create a profile for you, and determine whether they should lower your credit limit or raise your interest rate.

Charles Duhigg, a business reporter with *New York Times* **8** *Magazine*, published a fascinating article recently. He wrote that a math-loving analyst at Canadian Tire began to evaluate every piece of information they had collected from its credit card transactions that year. The analyst determined that the brands we buy were windows to our soul. For example, people who bought cheap, generic motor oil were more likely to miss a credit card payment than those who bought the more expensive brand-name oil. People who bought carbon monoxide detectors, premium birdseed, or felt pads for the bottom of furniture legs almost never missed payments. The reasoning—these people had a sense of responsibility toward the world, and wanted to protect their belongings, be it hardwood floors or credit ratings. On the other hand, people who bought chrome-skull car accessories or "mega thruster exhaust systems" were credit risks.

Hyper-targeting is the new 21st-century frontier in **9** marketing, because it delivers the two things advertisers have craved since the dawn of time—addressability and accountability. Some people are fine with giving away personal information on the Internet. As one friend said to me, it's the price of a free Google and Facebook. It's important, however, not to be apathetic about your data. If you understand how it all works, and where it's heading, at least you can begin to exert your own influence on the software engineers, financial statisticians, numerical analysts, and data scientists who are tracking you.

1085 words

Read the article and take detailed notes in the space provided.

1. What is hyper-targeting?	2. When, how, and why did hyper-targeting marketing evolve?	3. What are some examples of how we are being tracked online?	4. What can consumers do about target marketing?

Writing

Write a summary of the article "Hyper-Targeting: How Brands Track You Online." Your summary should be about 150-200 words. Refer to your notes above and the How To to help you write the summary.

✎ How To

WRITE A SUMMARY

When you summarize a text, you restate the main ideas and important details in a short form, using your own words.

1. Before you begin to write your summary, read and reread the original text very carefully to be sure you fully understand the main points and the important details.

2. Take notes as you read. Write your summary from your notes. (See the note-taking chart above.)

3. Begin your summary by identifying the title of the article, the author(s) name, and the main message of the article. For example:

   The article entitled _____, written by _____ , is about/describes/explains . . .

4. Then proceed to explain or describe each of the important details in logical order.

5. In summary writing you must use your own words as much as possible but you cannot include your own ideas or opinions.

6. If you use words from the original text, you must put quotation marks around them.

Focus on Language: Present Real Conditionals

Scan paragraph seven and fill in the missing verbs.

1. If you _____ using your credit card at second-hand stores, the credit card

   company _____ watching you.

2. If you _____ in to your credit card balance at one in the morning, it

   _____ sleeplessness due to financial anxiety.

3. If you _____ your balance three times a day, it _____ a warning

   signal.

4. How is the present real conditional formed?

   If + _____, _____

Discussion

1. Have you had any experiences online that indicated to you that advertisers were tracking you? If so, how did you react when you realized this was happening?

2. Should advertisers and marketers be allowed to track you online? If yes, what are the benefits of this form of marketing? If no, what can you do to prevent this form of virtual spying?

Topic Files

Topic Files Topic Files

Write a text or give an oral presentation about one of the following topics. Try to incorporate the elements seen in the unit from the Make the Connection box and use as many of the Top Words as you can, where appropriate.

Make the Connection

- ☐ Conditionals
- ☐ Vocabulary and idioms from the unit
- ☐ Pronouncing ordinal and cardinal numbers
- ☐ Thinking critically
- ☐ Writing a summary
- ☐ Writing an opinion essay

▶ **Refer to Writing Files 2, page 65, for information on essays.**

▶ **Refer to appendix 1, page 155, for information on oral presentations.**

1 MARKETING TO MILLENNIALS: What are the best ways for big companies to market their product to your generation? What type of ads work well for you? What types of ads do not?

2 COOLHUNTING: How far is too far? Big companies spend millions of dollars to search for what is cool and then market it to your generation. Is this fair advertising?

3 CAUSE MARKETING: Should all companies be encouraged to jump on the charity fund-raising bandwagon? Does cause marketing change your purchasing habits or how you feel about purchasing decisions?

4 COLOURS IN MARKETING: How does colour work at a subliminal level in advertising? How do colours influence what we wear, what we buy and how we feel?

5 HYPER-TARGET MARKETING: Have you ever noticed that companies or brands are hyper-targeting you? Describe how they do this. Do you think corporations have gone too far in tracking you online?

6 OTHER: _____ Write about another topic of your choice linked to what you learned in this unit. Make sure to have your topic approved by your teacher.

Top Words

Put a checkmark next to the words you know and refer to the page numbers to learn the ones you don't know. Add to the list other words that you want to remember from the unit.

ADJECTIVES
- ☐ **apathetic** (147)
- ☐ **aware** (135)
- ☐ **cheap** (135)
- ☐ **impressionable** (139)
- ☐ **relentless** (139)

NOUNS
- ☐ **advertising** (135)
- ☐ **a brand** (135)
- ☐ **a focus group** (135)
- ☐ **a marketer** (135)
- ☐ **a peer** (135)
- ☐ **a product** (135)
- ☐ **a value** (135)
- ☐ **worthiness** (147)

VERBS
- ☐ **to hire** (147)
- ☐ **to recognize** (139)
- ☐ **to target** (139)
- ☐ **to track** (147)
- ☐ **to utter** (147)

EXPRESSIONS
- ☐ **to back up** (135)
- ☐ **to be shut out** (135)

OTHER:

_____ _____

_____ _____

Vocabulary from the unit and other theme-related vocabulary can be practised online.

Vocabulary and Word Choice

Accurate word choice and the appropriate use of the language play major roles in creating a clear, interesting, and well-written document. This section focuses on aspects of vocabulary acquisition and word choice that will make you a better writer and make your texts more pleasurable to read.

Informal versus Standard English

Informal English is appropriate in casual conversation but you should avoid it in your essays and other formal academic writing.

- Do not use slang, or informal language.

  Informal *In today's consumer society, even **kids** think they need **lots of stuff**.*

  Standard *In today's consumer society, even **children** think they need **many possessions**.*

- Use standard verb forms.

Informal	Standard	Informal	Standard	Informal	Standard
~~ain't~~	is/am/are not	~~wanna~~	want to	~~woulda~~	would have
~~gonna~~	going to	~~gotta~~	have to	~~have gotta~~	have got to

- Do not use double negatives. Do not combine a negative word such as *no* or *nothing* with a negative adverb such as *not* or *never*.

Incorrect	Correct
~~He does not have no fun.~~	He has no fun. / He doesn't have any fun.
~~We didn't see nothing.~~	We didn't see anything.

Practice 1

Write a standard word that means the same as the common informal word.

Informal	Standard	Informal	Standard
1. awesome		**10.** fun	
2. boss		**11.** guys	
3. cash		**12.** hot	
4. cool		**13.** kids	
5. cops		**14.** job	
6. cute		**15.** stuff	
7. a fail		**16.** sucks	
8. for sure		**17.** tough	
9. freaked out		**18.** way better	

Edit the following paragraph. Find and correct or change four informal words, two non-standard verbs, and one double-negative.

Many people wanna be happier with their life. They spend large amounts of cash on insignificant stuff in the hopes that they will feel happiness. However, they gotta be careful what they wish for. People need to look beyond themselves and not become freaked out when they have one bad day. A more awesome quest would be to try to make a difference in the lives of others. This doesn't take no money at all and brings a much greater feeling of satisfaction.

Commonly Confused Words

Like most languages, English has many commonly confused words. Some of the confusion comes from homophones, which are words that are pronounced the same but have different meanings and spellings.

Practice 2

Look at this list of commonly confused words. Write the correct word in the sentence. Use your dictionary if you are not sure.

1. accept	except	Everyone _____ my brother is coming to the party.
2. advice	advise	I should listen to your _____ more often.
3. hear	listen	_____! Do you _____ a baby crying?
4. hole	whole	You should tell me the _____ story.
5. principal	principle	What is the _____ idea of this short story?
6. say	tell	Sarah _____ me you received 80% on your English exam.
7. succeed	success	I hope to have a lot of _____ in my life.
8. their	there	I put _____ books over _____, on the shelf.
9. weather	whether	Tell me _____ I should wear the red shoes or the black ones.
10. write	right	You are absolutely _____.

False Cognates

Cognates are words in different languages that share a similar meaning, spelling, and pronunciation. For example, the English noun *athlete* has the same meaning as the French noun *athlète* and the Spanish noun *atleta*.

False cognates are words that look similar in different languages but have different meanings. I ~~assisted~~ the conference. attended

Review this list of common false cognates. Avoid using these words incorrectly.

English / *French*	Meaning	Example
advertisement	A notice about something for sale	*There are too many advertisements in magazines.*
avertissement	A warning	*There is a severe weather warning. Be careful on the road.*
demand	To ask urgently for	*I demand that you tell me who stole my wallet.*
demander	To ask	*I asked the teacher a question about our homework.*
experience	An event in your life	*I had a wonderful experience in Greece this summer.*
expérience	An experiment	*The chemistry students conducted an experiment in class.*
formation	Structures or shapes	*Canada geese fly in a V formation.*
formation	Training/background	*Melissa has a background in social science.*
gentle	Tender temperament	*My kitten is so soft and gentle.*
gentil	Nice or kind	*Your sister is very nice to me.*
library	A place where you can borrow books	*I got some books at the library to help with my project.*
librairie	A bookstore	*I bought my books for English class at the bookstore.*
medicine	Drugs, mediation	*Don't forget to take your migraine medicine this morning.*
médecin	A doctor	*We see a doctor when we feel ill.*
publicity	The attention that someone or something gets from newspapers, television, the media	*The candidate for mayor got a lot of publicity for her alternative ideas.*
publicité	Advertisement	*Advertisements aimed at children should be limited.*

Practice 3

Underline and correct the false cognate in each sentence.

1. How much vacancy time do you get on your job? _____
2. I demanded that the teacher give me the homework. _____
3. Did you receive the publicity for the new gym? _____
4. It was very gentle of you to help me. _____
5. I have a formation in computer science. _____
6. I can't assist class today because I am sick. _____

The Academic Word List

The AWL is a list of words that are frequently found in English-language academic texts. Knowing these words will help you better understand academic texts in English. Using them in your writing will make your texts sound more academic.

Look at the words from the AWL taken from the units in the book. Check off the words you know and can use. Look up the unfamiliar words in a dictionary.

☐ to achieve (1)	☐ a bias (5)	☐ to enable (3)	☐ exposed (5)	☐ income (6)	☐ a purchase (6)
☐ accurate (5)	☐ bonding (6)	☐ an encounter (5)	☐ grades (2)	☐ overseas (3)	☐ to target (7)
☐ to be aware (7)	☐ to commit (4)				

Match each word from the AWL with its more common synonym. Try to use the
AWL words more often to make your essays sound more academic.

Academic Word		Common Word	Academic Word		Common Word
1. to pursue (v.)	(_____)	a. money	6. to acquire (v.)	(_____)	f. to happen
2. to occur (v.)	(_____)	b. simple	7. to survey (v.)	(_____)	g. to obtain
3. to achieve (v.)	(_____)	c. a situation	8. funds (n.)	(_____)	h. to help
4. to be aware (v.)	(_____)	d. to follow	9. an issue (n.)	(_____)	i. to accomplish
5. to aid (v.)	(_____)	e. to question	10. straightforward (adj.)	(_____)	j. to have knowledge

Use a Thesaurus

A thesaurus helps you avoid repetition in your writing and makes your writing more
vivid, interesting, and academic. Regular use of a thesaurus and dictionary will help
you increase your vocabulary and improve your written texts.

The common verb *see* can be replaced by *discover, notice, observe,* or *perceive*.

Practice 5

Replace the common vocabulary word in bold with a more descriptive word from
your thesaurus.

1. We **walked** leisurely through the park together. _____

2. She was so hungry; she **ate** all the food on her plate. _____

3. She got caught **sleeping** in class after a late night out. _____

4. He **made** dinner for his friends. _____

5. She **ran** so fast to catch the last train of the day. _____

Revise and Edit It!

Underline and correct the errors or problems in word choice in this passage. Make 10 corrections or changes.

Finding work that you are passionate about is a cool idea. A documentary about Sean Aiken

describes the adventure of a guy who worked 52 jobs in 52 weeks. Sean was not interested in

having tons of cash. He was more interested in finding his passion in life. When he graduated from

university with a formation in Business Administration, he didn't think nobody would wanna hire

him, but they did. In fact, he had all kinds of job offers for all kinds of jobs. His experiment was a

total succeed. At the end of his adventure, Sean learned that finding a passion is a continual

process. His advise to all is to be passionate about your life and your work. Sean is the real deal.

Appendix 1

How to Plan and Deliver an Oral Presentation

In this course, you often have to present information and opinions to your teacher and classmates orally. Speaking in front of others, especially in your second language, can be a challenge. The key is to be well prepared. Here are some helpful tips to make speaking in public easier.

Plan your presentation in advance

- Carefully review all of the requirements of the presentation.
- If you have to give a formal presentation, research and organize your ideas in the same way that you plan a written essay: an introduction, a few main points with support, and a conclusion.
- Incorporate new vocabulary and idioms.
- Be sure to use proper word stress and pronounce the verb endings clearly (-ed, -s, -ing).
- Practise your presentation aloud many times, preferably in front of someone who can suggest improvements.

- Time yourself to be sure your presentation meets the time limits set by your teacher.
- Prepare some simple cue cards with keywords to help your memory.
- Do not write down everything you want to say.
- Do not memorize your presentation word for word or you will sound stiff and unnatural.

Deliver your presentation with confidence

- Be enthusiastic about your topic and your ideas. Convey your enthusiasm in your voice and body language.
- Make regular eye contact with your teacher and audience.
- Speak clearly and at a natural speed (not too fast, and not too slow).
- Try to appear confident and comfortable.
- Do not read from your cue cards or from written documents.
- Bring in audio or visual support to make your presentation more interesting and memorable.

Appendix 2

How to Incorporate Research into Your College Assignments

In your English class it is often a requirement to incorporate research into your projects, presentations, and essays. There is so much information available that it can be a challenge to sort through it all, find what you need, and ensure that the information is relevant, interesting, and useful. Follow these steps to make sure that you use accurate and pertinent information in your assignments.

Step 1: Gather Your Research

1. Select and evaluate your research sources carefully

- Scan the headings and subheadings to ensure that the source is relevant.
- Check the date of publication to ensure that the source is current.

- Check the author and the title of publication to ensure that your source is reliable.
- Check for author bias.
- Do not assume that everything you read in a newspaper or online is reliable and relevant.
- Do not use commercial websites. They are not always reliable.
- Use the CARS checklist on the next page to validate Internet sources.

2. Take research notes

Once you have found useful sources, you need to record the relevant information.

- Take notes in point form in your own words.
- Record the information you will need for your list of references: author's name, title, date of publication, name of publisher, and website address.
- Use quotation marks to indicate the author's exact words.

	What to Validate	**Questions to Ask Yourself**
1. Credibility	Find out if the source is credible, or if you can trust it. Look for a reliable website and the person who wrote the material (institution, contact information, etc.).	Is the author respectable and well-known? Does the author have credentials? Does the website include the author's contact information? Is the information poorly written with a lot of mistakes?
2. Accuracy	Make sure that the article is up to date, detailed, and contains all the facts (the whole truth). Make sure that you know which audience the material is intended to reach. Look for a source that presents both sides of an issue (unbiased).	Is there a date? Do you know when it was last modified? Is the information intended for college students or higher? Does the author present both sides of an issue?
3. Reasonableness	Make sure that the information is fair and objective.	Is the writing very emotional? For example, a text from a vegetarians' association stating that eating meat is bad for you is probably biased. Does it make exaggerated claims? For example, a miracle cure for a problem should be approached with caution.
4. Support	Look for many sources that agree. Find sources that at least give similar information. Do not rely on one source only or on the first source that pops up.	Can you find three sources that agree?

Step 2: Incorporate Your Research

Incorporate research information into your assignments by summarizing, paraphrasing, or quoting directly. Make sure to record all your sources in a bibliography or reference section. Doing this will help you avoid plagiarism—presenting someone else's ideas as your own, in writing or orally.

1. Summarizing

The usual purpose of summarizing is to give the reader an overview of the text. To summarize information, find the main ideas in the text and rephrase them in your own words. Condense the most important ideas and state what you understand from them.

- Read the text carefully to ensure that you fully understand the information.
- Identify the title of the article you are summarizing, the author's name (if known), and the main idea in the first sentence of your summary.
- Acknowledge your source.
- Do not copy complete sentences directly from the article.

> "The Once-Over" by Carlin Flora, in Psychology Today, is about the importance and impact of first impressions. The author explains that we make a judgment about people in three seconds. These judgments are based on "thin slices" of information and are also influenced by the media and certain physical characteristics.

▷ For the full text, refer to unit 5 page 94.

2. Paraphrasing

To paraphrase, restate someone else's ideas in your own words without changing the original meaning. The usual purpose of paraphrasing is to express someone else's ideas more simply without using quotes.

- Read the text carefully to be sure you fully understand the information.
- Reword the author's ideas clearly and simply.
- Acknowledge your source.

> Helen Fisher explains that we are attracted to someone with a very different DNA from us in order to create genetic variety in our offspring. ("The Mysteries of Love")

▷ For the full text, refer to unit 4 pages 75-76, lines 27-28.

3. Quoting

Of the three ways to incorporate research into your assignments, quoting is the one you should use the least. Use quotes when the author wrote or said something in an eloquent, vivid, or memorable way that will add impact to your assignment.

- Copy the passage word for word from the original source.
- If the passage is shorter than 40 words, put quotation marks around it and incorporate it into your paragraph.
- If the passage is longer than 40 words, begin the quoted passage on a new line, indented ten spaces from the left margin.
- Acknowledge your source.

> To increase your level of happiness, laughing out loud is "the kind of adventurous, bold action that makes you feel happier," explains Will Fleeson PhD.

▷ For the full text, refer to unit 6 pages 125-126, lines 93-94.

4. Documenting your sources

Documentation is the process of acknowledging source material. To document a source, provide information that tells readers that certain ideas come from another writer. This allows them to find the source and read the material. When acknowledging your sources, follow an accepted format, such as the APA or MLA.

Step 3: Improve Your Research Assignment

Now that you have done your research and written a rough draft, it is time to revise, edit, and improve your work. Refer to the checklist at the back of the book to guide you in the revising and editing process.

Credits

Photo Sources

p. 1: Geber86/iStockphoto; **p. 3**: Deklofenak/iStockphoto; **p. 4**: pengpeng/iStockphoto; **p. 5**: lithian/Shutterstock; **p. 7**: diane39/iStockphoto; **p. 8**: Erik Khalitov/iStockphoto; **p. 10**: apomares/iStockphoto; **p. 11**: Lighthunter/Shutterstock; **p. 13**: 3dts/iStockphoto; **p. 14**: anzeletti/iStockphoto; **p. 16**: aslysun/Shutterstock; **p. 17**: difa/iStockphoto; **p. 19**: Kali Nine LLC/iStockphoto; **p. 27**: Juan Pablo Velaxo; **p. 28**: Sous la passerelle: Service de l'audiovisuel du Cégep Garneau; **p. 30**: olivier26/123RF Stock Photo; **p. 31**: Ian Campbell/CBC Still Photo Collection; **p. 32**: Squamish Lil'wat Cultural Centre; **p. 34**: JSummit Entertainment/Courtesy Everett Collection; **p. 37**: jonathansloane/iStockphoto; **p. 39**: Joey Boylan/iStockphoto; **p. 41**: Jodi Cobb/National Geographic Society/Corbis; **p. 42**: Jodi Cobb/National Geographic Society/Corbis; **p. 43**: Jodi Cobb/National Geographic; **p. 45**: © Stefania Besca/Flickr/Getty Images; **p. 46**: Robert Churchill/iStockphoto; **p. 48 (1)**: Magnus Kallstrom/Shutterstock, **(2)**: Khoroshunova Olga/Shutterstock, **(3)**: Telegin Sergey/Shutterstock, **(4)**: Mark Yuill/Shutterstock, **(5)**: Avatar_023/Shutterstock, **(6)**: ArtmannWitte/iStockphoto; **p. 49**: Rex Pemberton; **p. 50**: Rajesh_KC/iStockphoto; **p. 51**: Tori Holmes; **p. 53**: DHuss/iStockphoto; **p. 56 (1)**: Outpost Magazine, **(2)**: Outpost Magazine; **p. 57**: Outpost Magazine; **p. 58 (1)**: Outpost Magazine, **(2)**: Outpost Magazine; **p. 60**: Rasica/iStockphoto; **p. 61**: Alexandra Liss of www.OneCouchataTime.com; **p. 62**: AfricaImages/iStockphoto; **p. 71**: Jodi Cobb/National Geographic Creative; **p. 72**: kevinruss/iStockphoto; **p. 73**: Richard Olsenius/National Geographic Creative; **p. 74**: Anna Bryukhanova/iStockphoto; **p. 75**: Mediaphotos/iStockphoto; **p. 77**: lentolo/iStockphoto; **p. 78**: Digital Innovations Group, Inc and Robert Kenner Films; **p. 82 (1)**: FeyginFoto/Shutterstock, **(2)**: Maridav/Shutterstock, **(3)**: Kinga/Shutterstock; **p. 83**: Lisa-Blue/iStockphoto; **p. 84**: Jodi Cobb/National Geographic Creative; **p. 86**: CBS/Landov; **p. 91**: Kokkai Ng; **p. 92**: Warren Goldswain/Shutterstock; **p. 94**: whitetag/iStockphoto; **p. 96**: mediaphotos/iStockphoto; **p. 97**: Anastasia Alexandrova/Thinkstock; **p. 98**: Mac99/iStockphoto; **p. 99**: Ajkkafe/iStockphoto; **p. 100**: Denis Mironov/Shutterstock; **p. 101**: scyther5/Shutterstock; **p. 102**: michaeljung/Shutterstock; **p. 103**: istockphoto via Thinkstock; **p. 105**: TonyYao/Thinkstock; **p. 106**: Purestock/Thinkstock; **p. 113**: © Liesl Marelli; **p. 114 (1)**: Goodluz/Thinkstock, **(2)**: Alexander Kalina/Shutterstock, **(3)**: Devonyu/iStockphoto, **(4)**: Devonyu/iStockphoto; **p. 115 (1)**: MorePixels/iStockphoto, **(2)**: bizoo_n/iStockphoto; **p. 117**: kutaytanir/iStockphoto; **p. 118**: Mikadun/Shutterstock; **p. 120 (1)**: JcJg Photography/Fotolia, **(2)**: PhotosbyAbby/iStockphoto, **(3)**: WendellandCarolyn/iStockphoto, **(4)**: Rogério Bernardo/Dreamstime, **(5)**: EMPPhotography/iStockphoto, **(6)**: Xtremepixel/Dreamstime; **p. 121**: OneWeekJob.com; **p. 123**: OneWeekJob.com; **p. 125**: YanLev/Shutterstock; **p. 127**: Caialmage/iStockphoto; **p. 129**: ferrantraite/iStockphoto; **p. 131**: AleksandarNakic/iStockphoto; **p. 134**: Catherine Yeulet/Thinkstock; **p. 135**: Yongyuan Dai/iStockphoto; **p. 137**: bulentozber/iStockphoto; **p. 139**: a-wrangler/iStockphoto; **p. 140**: Ryan McVay/Thinkstock; **p. 141 (1)**: nicolas/iStockphoto, **(2)**: fotohunter/Shutterstock, **(3)**: Africa Studio/Shutterstock, **(4)**: MNStudio/Shutterstock; **p. 142**: leolintang /iStockphoto; **p. 144**: Bart Sadowski/iStockphoto; **p. 147**: hidesy/iStockphoto; **p. 149**: Enviromantic/iStockphoto; **p. 156**: Tarik Kizilkaya/iStockphoto.

Text, Audio, and Video Sources

Unit 1, p. 4 Reading text: "Video Games: An Hour a Day Is Key to Success in Life" by Jane McGonigal, *Huffington Post* ©2011; **p. 7 Video segment**: "Texting: Can We Pull the Plug On Our obsession?" CBS News ©2012; **p. 8 Reading text**: "Ten Big Ways the Internet Is Changing Our Brains" www.onlinecollege.org ©2012; **p. 11 Video segment**: "Facebook Follies," CBC ©2012; **p. 17 Reading text**: "The Flight From Conversation" by Sherry Turkle, *New York Times* ©2012; **Unit 2, p. 29 Reading text**: "Who Am I?" by Julia Belluz, *Maclean's* ©2010; **p. 31 Video segment**: "8th Fire: It's Time!" CBC ©2011; **p. 34 Reading text**: *The Perks of Being a Wallflower* Reprinted with the permission of Gallery Publishing Group from the Pocket Book edition of *The Perks of Being a Wallflower* by Stephen Chbosky. Copyright © 1999 by Stephen Chbosky. All rights reserved. **p. 39 Audio segment**: "The Sibling Effect" adapted from NPR's "On Point" produced by WBUR, Boston, MA, USA; **p. 41 Reading text**: "A Thing or Two About Twins" by Peter Miller, *National Geographic* ©2012; **Unit 3, p. 48 Video segment**: *Skyward Journey* by Rex Pemberton, RPMP; **p. 51 Reading text**: "I Want to Row Across the Atlantic" by Tori Holmes ©2012; **p. 55 Reading text**: "Travellers for Change," *Outpost Magazine* ©2007; **p. 61 Video segment**: "One Couch at a Time" www.onecouchatatime.com/©2013; **Unit 4, p. 75 Reading text**: "The Mysteries of Love" by Sara Reistad-Long, *Real Simple* ©2007 Time Inc. All rights reserved. Reprinted from *Real Simple* and published with permission of Time Inc. Reproduction in any manner in any language in whole or in part without written permission is prohibited; **p. 78 Video segment**: *When Strangers Click* ©MMX Robert Kenner Films and Digital Innovations Group; **p. 82 Reading text**: "Love Types" by Dr. Helen Fisher ©2007 www.oprah.com; **p. 84 Video segment**: *That Thing Called Love*, *National Geographic* ©2006; **p. 87 Reading text**: "The Chaser" by John Collier, *The New Yorker* ©1940; **Unit 5, p. 94 Reading text**: "The Once-Over" by Carlin Flora, *Psychology Today* ©2004; **p. 99 Video segment**: "Borrow a Stereotype", CBC News Sunday ©2008; **p. 102 Reading text**: "Women and Math" adapted from "False Stereotypes Can Affect Performance: B.C. Study", CBC News ©2006; **p. 103 Reading text**: "Beauty Bias" adapted from "First Impressions Of Beauty May Demonstrate Why The Pretty Prosper", *Science Daily* ©2006; **p. 105 Audio segment**: "The Gender Trap" with Paul Kennedy, CBC Radio: Ideas ©2012; **Unit 6, p. 117 Reading text**: "Money Can Buy You Happiness–If You Spend It on Others", CBC News ©2008; **p. 118 Reading text**: "Study: Experiences Make Us Happier than Possessions" by Elizabeth Landau, CNN ©2009; **p.121 Reading text**: "My Generation" by Sean Aiken ©www.oneweekjob.com; **p. 123 Video segment**: *One-Week Job* by Sean Aiken and Ian MacKenzie, Metta Films ©www.oneweekjob.com; **p. 125 Reading text**: "The Way to Happiness" by Dianne Hales, *Reader's Digest* ©2008; **p. 128 Video segment**: "Laughter Is the Best Medicine", CTV Montreal News ©2012; **Unit 7, p. 134 Reading text**: "Marketing to Millennials" by Ripley Daniels socialmediatoday.com ©2012; **p. 139 Video segment**: "Hunting for Cool" adapted from "The Merchants of Cool", Frontline, WGBH Boston, PBS ©2001; **p. 142 Reading text**: "Pink Ribbon Green" by Dan Delmar, Special to *The Suburban* ©2010; **p. 144 Audio segment**: "How Colour Makes Us Buy" adapted from "Colour Schemes: How Colour Makes us Buy" with Terry O'Reilly, Under the Influence, CBC Radio ©2013; **p. 147 Reading text**: "Hyper-Targeting: How Brands Track You Online" with Terry O'Reilly, Under the Influence, CBC Radio ©2012.